SERIES XXXIV NO. 2

JOHNS HOPKINS UNIVERSITY STUDIES
IN
HISTORICAL AND POLITICAL SCIENCE
Under the Direction of the
Departments of History, Political Economy, and Political Science

THE POSTAL POWER OF CONGRESS

A STUDY IN CONSTITUTIONAL EXPANSION

BY

LINDSAY ROGERS, Ph.D., LL.B.
Adjunct Professor of Political Science in the University of Virginia

THE LAWBOOK EXCHANGE, LTD.
Clark, New Jersey
2006

ISBN-13: 978-1-58477-677-2
ISBN-10: 1-58477-677-3

Printed in the United States of America on acid-free paper

THE LAWBOOK EXCHANGE, LTD.
33 Terminal Avenue
Clark, New Jersey 07066-1321

Please see our website for a selection of our other publications and fine facsimile reprints of classic works of legal history:
www.lawbookexchange.com

Library of Congress Cataloging-in-Publication Data

Rogers, Lindsay, 1891-1970.
The postal power of Congress : a study in constitutional expansion / Lindsay Rogers.
p. cm.
Originally published: Baltimore: Johns Hopkins Press, 1916, in series: John Hopkins University Studies in historical and political science. Series XXXIV, no. 2.
Includes bibliographical references and index.
ISBN-13: 978-1-58477-677-2 (alk. paper)
ISBN-10: 1-58477-677-3 (alk. paper)
1. Postal service--United States--History. 2. Postal service--Law and legislation--United States. 3. United States. Congress--Powers and duties. I. Title.
HE6371.R7 2006
343.7309'92--dc22 2006018813

SERIES XXXIV **NO. 2**

JOHNS HOPKINS UNIVERSITY STUDIES

IN

HISTORICAL AND POLITICAL SCIENCE

Under the Direction of the

Departments of History, Political Economy, and
Political Science

THE POSTAL POWER OF CONGRESS

A STUDY IN CONSTITUTIONAL EXPANSION

BY

LINDSAY ROGERS, Ph.D., LL.B.

Adjunct Professor of Political Science in the University of Virginia

---

BALTIMORE

THE JOHNS HOPKINS PRESS

1916

PRESS OF
THE NEW ERA PRINTING COMPANY
LANCASTER, PA.

CONTENTS

PREFACE

The purpose of this essay is to trace the legislative and judicial history of the grant to Congress of the power "to establish postoffices and postroads," and to discuss the constitutionality of the proposals that, under this clause, federal control may be extended to subjects over which Congress has no direct authority. The essay is thus one in constitutional expansion, and does not consider the history or efficiency of the postoffice as an administrative arm of the government. A treatment of this subject, which has as yet received scant notice, I may some day attempt.

Portions of Chapters IV and VII have appeared as articles on "Federal Interference with the Freedom of the Press," and "The Extension of Federal Control through the Regulation of the Mails," in the *Yale Law Journal* (May, 1914) and the *Harvard Law Review* (November, 1913) respectively. They have been thoroughly revised for publication in their present form. Chapter V appeared in substantially the same form in the *Virginia Law Review* (November, 1915).

I am under great obligations to Professor W. W. Willoughby, not only for much direct assistance in the preparation of this essay, but for the inspiration of his productive scholarship.

L. R.

THE POSTAL POWER OF CONGRESS

CHAPTER I

INTRODUCTORY: THE ANTECEDENTS OF THE POWER

It is, perhaps, not insignificant that *The Federalist* contains but a single reference to the power lodged in Congress "to establish postoffices and postroads." The writers of that incomparable collection of political papers which discussed in such exhaustive detail the disputed points of the proposed governmental frame-work for the United States of America, hardly needed to argue that the proposed delegation could not be deemed dangerous and was admittedly one of national concern. "The power of establishing postroads," said Madison, "must, in every view, be a harmless power, and may, perhaps, by judicious management, become productive of great public conveniency. Nothing which tends to facilitate the intercourse between the states can be deemed unworthy of the public care."[1]

Half a century later, Story prefaced the discussion of this power in his *Commentaries,* with the remark that, "One cannot but feel, at the present time, an inclination to smile at the guarded caution of these expressions, and the hesitating avowal of the importance of the power. It affords, perhaps, one of the most striking proofs, how much the growth and prosperity of the country have outstripped the most sanguine anticipations of our most enlightened patriots."[2]

At the time Story wrote, the postal power had, of course, already achieved a "commercial, political, intellectual and

[1] The Federalist, No. 42.
[2] Story, Commentaries on the Constitution, vol. iii, p. 22.

private" importance, "of incalculable value to the permanent interests of the Union," vital both to the government and to individuals. But there was also the problem, lately acute, as to whether Congress had simply the power "to designate, or point out, what roads shall be mail roads, and the right of passage or way along them when so designated," or the larger power "to construct any roads which Congress may deem proper for the conveyance of the mail, and to keep them in due repair for such purpose."[3] The remarkable benefits already achieved and the disputed extensions were the developments which excited Story's surprise at the unprophetic remark of *The Federalist*.

But for some time the postoffice has been a common carrier and is now supplanting the express companies; it exercises banking functions not only for facilitating exchange but for savings deposits, and other collectivist activities are most strongly urged. The Supreme Court of the United States has upheld a broad power in Congress to prevent and punish interference with the carriage of the mails, and it is thus possible to make further extensions of federal authority.[4] The right to incorporate railways and build postroads is firmly established, and assertions are made that it is both competent and advisable for federal authority to assume control of the telephone and telegraph systems and perhaps the railways themselves. It is, finally, argued that Congress may solve problems of purely local origin, and of primary sectional concern, through the simple expedient of denying the use of the mails unless certain regulative conditions are complied with. Viewing these extensions as either definitely upheld by the Supreme Court, or seriously urged, one cannot now but smile at the "guarded caution" of Story's description and his "hesitating avowal" that postroads might, with certain restrictions, be constructed under federal auspices. The distinguished jurist, however, wrote more prophetically than he knew, when he empha-

[3] Story, Commentaries on the Constitution, vol. iii, p. 26.
[4] In Re Debs, 158 U. S. 564 (1895).

sized the importance of this power, "both theoretically and practically."

Yet it is not unnatural that at the time the Constitution was framed, the importance of the postal power should have been inadequately estimated, since, inherently, it must be conditioned by the existing mechanical means of intercourse and communication. It seemed that the nation would be sufficiently fortunate were it to be born with promise of maintaining existence, and it was neither possible nor advisable to scrutinize its powers of which future necessity or expediency might require an extension for the purposes of the nation. And, moreover, the growth of postal facilities, from their first manifestation up to the adoption of the Constitution was not sufficiently pronounced to augur a great deal for the future. Travel and intercourse were extremely difficult; and the cognate questions were to come only with the development of society.

The maintenance of postal facilities has always been a recognized function of the state, and this was true even in early Rome. In England, the sixteenth century saw the first definite steps for the establishment of a service, but even before this communications were carried by royal messengers compensated by the Crown. Private posts were, of course, used, but official letters on state matters constituted so large a bulk of the correspondence and the problem was one so fitted for solution by the state that it was inevitable that the postal establishment should be conducted under the auspices of, and supported directly by the government.[5]

In the American colonies the first attempt to establish a mail service was made in 1639 by the General Court of Massachusetts. "For preventing the miscarriage of letters, . . . It is ordered that notice bee given, that Richard Fairbanks, his house in Boston, is the place appointed for all letters, which are brought from beyond the seas, or are to bee sent thither; . . . are to bee brought to him and hee is to

[5] Hemmeon, The History of the British Post Office, p. 3 ff.

take care, that they bee delivered or sent according to their directions and hee is allowed for every such letter 1*d.* and must answer for all miscarriages through his owne neglect in this kind; provided no man shall bee compelled to bring his letters thither except hee please." So runs the entry in the court records.[6]

This, however, applied only to foreign mail, and it was not until December, 1672 that there was an effort to establish a domestic post, Francis Lovelace, governor of New York, taking the initiative, and his messenger going to Connecticut. Soon afterwards the General Court of Massachusetts appointed a postmaster and a proclamation was issued by the home government calling for the establishment of postoffices at convenient places on the American continent.[7]

The office of postmaster general for America was created in 1692, permission being granted Thomas Neale and his executors by the Lords of Trade and Plantations to establish "an office or offices for the receiving and dispatching letters and pacquets, and to receive, send and deliver the same under such rates and sums as the planters shall agree to give."[8]

The next forty years saw some extensions of postal facilities, but the improvement was slight. In 1683 William Penn established a postoffice in Pennsylvania, and in 1736 a weekly mail was begun between Boston and New York, but intercolonial communication was very restricted, and it was not until 1737, with the appointment of Benjamin Franklin as postmaster general at Philadelphia and postmaster general of the Colonies in 1753 that there were any noticeable gains, or any signs of important developments

[6] Mass. Historical Collections, 3d Series, vol. vii, p. 48; quoted by Mary E. Wooley in her monograph on "Early History of the Colonial Post Office," Publications of the Rhode Island Historical Society, New Series, vol. i, p. 270 ff.

[7] Hemmeon, p. 32; Joyce, The History of the Post Office from its Establishment down to 1836, p. 196.

[8] Wooley, Early History of the Colonial Post Office, p. 275; Hemmeon, p. 33. See also Pliny Miles, "History of the Post Office," American Bankers' Magazine, n. s., vol. vii, p. 358 (November, 1857).

for the state function of which he was placed in charge. Franklin was active in establishing new posts as far as was possible and began the practice of sending newspapers through the mails free of charge. When he was turned out of office in 1774, he wrote that "before I was displaced by a freak of the ministers, we had brought it [the postoffice] to yield three times as much clear revenue to the crown as the postoffice in Ireland. Since that impudent transaction they have received from it not one farthing."[9]

After Franklin's dismissal the new postmaster at Philadelphia raised the rates on newspapers to such proportions that William Goddard, an editor of Baltimore and Philadelphia, was forced to discontinue the publication of his journal. In March, 1774 Goddard began a lengthy journey through the New England States to gain support for the "Constitutional American Post Office" which he hoped to establish.[10] A tentative line was inaugurated between Baltimore and Philadelphia, but this was gradually extended so as to provide tolerably adequate facilities for all of the colonies, Goddard having secured the support of the assemblies in New Hampshire, Massachusetts, Rhode Island, New Jersey, and New York.[11] He realized from the first that the facilities he was seeking should be furnished under the auspices of the Continental Congress, and when this body acted on July 26, 1775 and agreed to the establishment of a post, Goddard's plans were accepted.[12]

The establishment of postal facilities was one of the very first problems taken up by the Continental Congress when it began to exercise sovereign powers which it did not legally possess, but which of necessity it had to assume. On May 29, 1775 the Congress resolved that, "As the present critical situation of the colonies renders it highly desirable that ways and means should be devised for the speedy and secure conveyance of Intelligence from one end

[9] Miles, p. 361.
[10] American Archives, Fourth Series, vol. i, pp. 500–504.
[11] Ibid., vol. ii, p. 536 ff.
[12] See Jameson (Ed.), Essays in Constitutional History, p. 168 ff.

of the Continent to the other," a committee be appointed to consider the best means of establishing a post,[13] and on July 26, 1775 the Congress took up the committee's report, appointed Benjamin Franklin postmaster general for the United Colonies, established a line of communication from Falmouth to Savannah and recommended the inauguration of cross posts within the discretion of the postmaster general.[14] Franking privileges were almost immediately established for the members of Congress and for the army commanders, and were later extended, with some limitations, to private soldiers in the service.[15]

As yet the Congress had not aimed to make its postal establishment a monopoly and so it was a question of war policy rather than of the unrestricted exercise of a governmental function which inspired the motion that the parliamentary posts be stopped. Richard Henry Lee, for example, argued that "the Ministry are mutilating our correspondence in England, and our enemies here are corresponding for our ruin;" but the better opinion prevailed that the measure was an offensive one not proper at that particular juncture. In fact the ministerial post had been of service to the colonists in giving them information which they could not otherwise have obtained, and so it was recommended that the people use the constitutional establishment as much as possible. Before the end of the year, as it turned out, this problem was settled without the intervention of Congress for the British postoffice stopped its service in the colonies.[16]

---

[13] Journals of the Continental Congress (edited by Ford), ii, p. 71. (References up to 1781 are to this edition, Washington, 1904 . . . Since the sixteenth volume, the editor has been Gaillard Hunt.)

[14] Ibid., vol. ii, p. 208.

[15] Ibid., vol. iii, p. 342; vol. iv, p. 43.

[16] Ibid., vol. iii, p. 488. In the discussion referred to Paine remarked that the "ministerial post will die a natural death; it has been under a languishment a great while; it would be cowardice to issue a decree to kill that which is dying; it brought but one letter last time and was obliged to retail newspapers to pay its expenses." Lee was more facetious, saying: "Is there not a Doctor, Lord North, who can keep this creature alive?" On December 25, 1775, it was announced that incoming mail would not be sent to the various colonies but would be held in New York and advertised.

During the war the adequacy of the postal facilities was often before Congress. Committees were appointed to investigate conditions; Congress by resolution appreciated the fact that the "communication of intelligence with frequency and despatch from one part to another of this extensive continent, is essentially requisite to its safety." The postmaster general was therefore requested to exercise care in the selection of riders and to discharge dilatory ones when discovered. Deputy postmasters were excused "from those public duties which may call them from attendance at their offices;" admonitory resolutions directed ferry keepers to expedite the passage of postriders, and a public monopoly was aimed at through the indirect method of reducing the wages of government messengers who carried private packages.[17]

On November 7, 1776, Richard Bache was appointed postmaster general vice Franklin who had gone on the mission to France, and after this change the attempts of Congress to improve the service seem to be more frequent.[18] In January of the next year, Bache was requested to furnish a list of those in the service, it having been reported that "persons disaffected to the American cause" had been employed "with the most mischievous effects" and he was further requested to "assign reasons why the late resolves of Congress for regulating the postoffice are not carried into execution."[19] In February a committee was appointed to revise the regulations; it recommended extensions and suggested that all employees be required to take an "oath of fidelity to the United States and also an oath of office," and urged that once in six months the postmaster general be required to transmit to Congress a list of those in the service.[20] The legislatures of the states were asked to exempt from all military duties "persons immediately con-

[17] Journals of the Continental Congress, vol. v, pp. 719, 720; vi, p. 926.
[18] Ibid., vol. vi, p. 931.
[19] Ibid., vol. vii, p. 29.
[20] Ibid., p. 153.

cerned in conducting the business of the postoffice," but still the establishment did not work to the satisfaction of Congress, and other committees were appointed to make recommendations and the rates of postage were several times increased. One new step was taken when an inspector of dead letters was appointed to "examine all dead letters at the expiration of each quarter; to communicate to Congress such letters as contain inimical schemes or intelligence; to preserve carefully all money, loan office certificates, lottery tickets, notes of hand, and other valuable papers enclosed in any of them, and be accountable" for their safekeeping, subject to the restriction that he take "no copy of any letter whatever," and refuse "to divulge their contents to any but Congress or those whom they may appoint for the purpose."[21]

Meanwhile the Articles of Confederation had been agreed upon and submitted to the states. There was no objection to a grant of the postal power, but the terms in which it was made limited its extent. Part of Article XVIII in the first draft gave the United States "the sole and exclusive right and power of . . . establishing and regulating postoffices throughout all the United Colonies, on lines of communication from one colony to another," and later on in the same article, it was provided that the United States "shall never impose or levy any taxes or duties except in managing the postoffice."[22] In the second draft, the grant was made more limited; it gave Congress "the sole and exclusive right and power . . . of establishing and regulating postoffices from one state to another throughout all the United States and exacting such postage on the papers passing through the same as may be requisite to defray the expenses of said office." In this form the clause became part of the Articles of Confederation as adopted by the states,[23] and there was no further discussion of the power,

[21] Journals of the Continental Congress, vol. vii, pp. 258, 347; ix, 816, 817, 898; xi, 550.

[22] Ibid., vol. v, p. 551.

[23] Ibid., pp. 681, 682; ix, 907. In the second draft the postal clause comes under Article 14 and in the final draft under Article 9.

negative action being taken on the motion of the Pennsylvania delegates (June 25, 1778) "that such part of the 9th article as respects the postoffice, be altered or amended so as that Congress be obliged to lay the accounts annually before the legislatures of the several states."[24]

The Articles of Confederation gave the limited power of establishing and regulating postoffices "from one state to another." Thus, intrastate postal facilities were beyond the purview of Congress; nothing was said, moreover, about the establishment of postroads, or the opening up of new routes, and the sole power of taxation granted to Congress was confined to an amount sufficient to defray the expenses of the system. Nevertheless, the inadequacy of the grant was theoretical rather than real, since Congress was so occupied with other more pressing affairs, that it was content with a limited communication of intelligence, desiring solely that this be as speedy and secure as possible.

From this time on references to the postal establishment in the congressional journals are of frequent occurrence; additional investigating committees were established and the personnel of the standing committee was changed. Expenses grew apace while the revenues diminished and this called for measures of retrenchment. A resolution of December 27, 1779, contained the regulation that "the post shall set out and arrive at the place where Congress shall be sitting twice in every week," and it was at the same time urged that "the whole expensive system of express riding be totally abolished except by the particular order of Congress upon very special occasions."[25]

On October 18, 1782, under the power granted by the Articles of Confederation, there was passed "An Ordinance for Regulating the Post-Office of the United States of America." For the period it was a most elaborate statute and marks the birth of a real postal establishment. Of such

[24] Journals of the Continental Congress, vol. xi, p. 652. The vote stood, Ayes, 2; Noes, 9.

[25] Ibid., vol. xv, p. 1411.

comprehensiveness was the act that when, ten years later, Congress passed legislation under the authority delegated by the Constitution, the Ordinance was merely amplified. Its preamble recited:

"Whereas the communication of intelligence with regularity and dispatch from one part to another of these United States is essentially requisite to the safety as well as the commercial interest thereof; and the United States in Congress assembled being by the Articles of Confederation vested with the sole and exclusive right and power of establishing and regulating postoffices throughout all these United States; and whereas it is become necessary to revise the several regulations heretofore made relating to the postoffice and reduce to one act:

"Be it therefore ordained by the United States in Congress assembled, and it is hereby ordained by the authority of the same, that a continued communication of posts throughout these United States shall be established and maintained by and under the direction of the postmaster general of these United States to extend to and from the state of New Hampshire to the state of Georgia inclusive, and to and from such other parts of the United States as from time to time he shall judge necessary or Congress shall direct."[26]

The duties of the postmaster general were "to superintend and direct the postoffice in all its various departments and services . . . agreeably to the rules and regulations" of the ordinance. He was given the power to appoint an assistant and deputies, for whom he should be responsible; to station them, and to fix their commissions, with a maximum limit of 20 per cent. on money "to arise from postage in their respective departments." He was given the further power of appointing postriders, messengers and expresses.

In this ordinance, moreover, Congress attempted to lay down certain regulations, infraction of which would be punishable, although not criminally or in an efficient manner. All persons in the service were forbidden knowingly or

[26] 7 Journals of Congress (Ed. of 1800), 383.

wilfully "to open, detain, delay, secrete, embezzle, or destroy, or cause, procure, permit, or suffer to be opened, detained, delayed, secreted, embezzled or destroyed, any letter or letters, packet or packets, or other dispatch or dispatches, which shall come into his power, hands, or custody, by reason of his employment in, or relation to, the post-office, except by the consent of the person or persons by or to whom the same shall be delivered or directed, or by an express warrant under the hand of the president of the Congress of these United States or in time of war, of the commander in chief of the armies of these United States, or of the chief executive officer of one of the said states, for that purpose, or except in such other cases wherein he shall be authorized to do so by this ordinance."

All persons in the postal service were required, antecedent to their employment, to take an oath promising to carry out and obey these meticulous provisions to safeguard the mails, but the method of enforcement was ineffective. Congress provided that "if the postmaster general shall be guilty of the said oath or affirmation or any part thereof, and be thereof convict, he shall forfeit and pay 1,000 dollars in an action of debt in the state where the offense shall be committed, by the treasurer of the United States for the time being." The penalty for other employees was $300, but all were "rendered incapable ever hereafter of holding any office or place of trust or profit under these United States."[27]

In order to make probable a higher degree of efficiency and to insure adequate revenues, the Congress attempted to make and enforce a monopoly. The Ordinance specified that the postmaster and his assistants, but "no other person whatsoever shall have the receiving, taking up, ordering, dispatching . . . carrying and delivering of any letters, packets or other dispatches, from any place within these United States for hire, reward, or other profit or advantage . . . and any such person or persons presuming to do so,

[27] 7 Journals, 383 ff. Special messengers and expresses were exempted from this provision at the discretion of the postmaster general.

shall forfeit and pay for every such offense, 20 dollars, to be sued for and recovered in an action of debt with costs of the suit." Persons on private missions were exempted and private cross posts could be established with the approval of the postmaster general. By the ordinance rates were fixed and special provisions were made for newspapers which were to be carried "at such moderate rates as the postmaster general shall establish." The franking privilege, finally, was extended to the officials at Washington and single letters could be sent without postage to officers of the line in actual service; by early amendments to the ordinance there were further extensions, Washington was relieved of paying postage and allowance was made for ministers at foreign courts.[28]

The incompleteness of the national control over the post-office and in particular the inadequacy of the device that really criminal offenses should be punished by civil suits, were shown in January, 1784 when Congress considered a robbery which had taken place at Princeton. The mail had been carried off and some days later was found in a meadow, several letters having been lost and several more, franked by members of Congress, having been broken open. The "supreme executive of the state of New Jersey" was requested to undertake an investigation to discover those guilty, but when his reply exculpated the Princeton postmaster "from every suspicion of collusion or fraud" the inquiry was dropped. Congress could proceed no further.[29]

Another incident showing general acceptance of the fact that the regulation of the mails and the punishment of offenses against them should be under plenary national control, occurred a few months later and was considered by the Committee of the States during a recess of Congress. An investigating committee reported that an advertisement of French packet boats was "an open avowal of an intention to contravene an ordinance of Congress for regulating

[28] 8 Journals, 40, 131, 193; 9 Journals, 130.
[29] 9 Journals, 15, 147.

the postoffice of these United States; and that the measures therein mentioned . . . are a flagrant violation of the same ordinance . . . will greatly injure the revenue of the post-office, and, if not prevented, may defeat that useful institution." The Committee of the States agreed to the report and directed that if the postmaster general should determine that the ordinance had been violated, he should cause the prosecution of the offenders according to law, namely, make them defendants in actions of debt for the penalties provided by the ordinance.[30]

On September 4, the postmaster general was given authority to contract for the conveyance of the mails by stage carriages, if practicable, for one year, but on the part of some of the states considerable opposition developed. A motion was made to construe the words "if practicable" as not binding the postoffice "to form the contract for the transportation of the mail on terms inconvenient to the mercantile interest, or to comply with the extravagant demands of the contractors," but the vote was in the negative and a second attempt to modify the original instruction was also unsuccessful.[31] The later motion showed a disposition on the part of the states to desire flexible national regulations, which would not necessarily be uniform, but would be adapted to local needs. The resolution recited that in respect to the states of New Jersey, Pennsylvania, Delaware, Maryland and Virginia, the mails might "be carried upon more reasonable and convenient terms should the postmaster general be left at liberty to contract for the same either by stage carriages or postriders, as shall appear to him most conducive to the public interest.

"And whereas the intention of Congress in having the mail transported by stage carriages was not only to render their conveyance more certain and secure, but by encouraging the establishment of stages to make intercourse between different parts of the union less difficult and expensive than

[30] 9 Journals (App.), 10.
[31] 11 Journals, 154, 191.

formerly; and as a discretionary power in the postmaster general either to employ postriders or contract with the owners of stage carriages for conveying the mail in the states of North Carolina, South Carolina, and Georgia might interfere with the object of promoting and establishing the running of stages in said states, Resolved, that so far as respects these states it is improper to alter the postmaster general's present instructions."[32] Thus very early attempts were made to secure special local facilities.

During this period, however, subsequent to the ordinance of 1782, Congress took no important action in regard to the postoffice. It annually gave the postmaster general authority to contract for the succeeding year, and to encourage the useful institution of the postoffice when it could be done without material injury to the public.[33] In the enforcement of federal regulations, as has been said, the government was limited by having to sue in actions of debt, and so it was a foregone conclusion that the postal power, inadequately vested in Congress under the Articles of Confederation, would be one of the grants contained in the Constitution. The Pinckney plan as it was submitted to the Committee of Detail, mentioned "establishing Post-Offices" as one of the exclusive powers of "the Senate and House of Delegates in Congress assembled."[34] Pinckney's original draft outlined the power as that "of establishing Post-Offices and raising a revenue from them."[35]

In the Convention Mr. Paterson on June 15, 1787 sug-

---

[32] Congress approved the action of the postmaster general in directing his deputies not to receive the paper money of any state for postage, and to accept only specie. He was also authorized to demand payment in advance. 11 Journals, 84, 164.

[33] 12 Journals, 137.

[34] Farrand, Records of the Federal Convention, vol. ii, p. 135.

[35] This is the draft as reconstructed by Professor Farrand (vol. iii, pp. 604, 607), but the document sent by Pinckney in 1819 to John Quincy Adams for publication in the journal, omitted the last clause. This draft, however, was written not very long before 1819, and was not presented to the Convention in 1787. See Records, vol. iii, p. 595 ff; "Sketch of Pinckney's Plan for a Constitution, 1787," in American Historical Review, vol. ix, p. 735, and Bancroft, History of the Constitution, vol. i, p. 258.

gested "that in addition to the power vested in the United States by the existing articles of Confederation, they be authorized to pass acts for raising a revenue, . . . by a postage on all letters and packages passing through the general postoffice, to be applied to such federal purposes as they shall deem proper and expedient."[36] The report of the Committee of Detail was made to the Convention on August 6 and provided (Art. VII) that "The Legislature of the United States shall have the power . . . to establish postoffices."[37]

Ten days later, the Committee's report being under consideration it was proposed that the words "and postroads" be added. This was carried by a close vote, though it is difficult to attribute the opposition to any source other than a general fear of giving the federal government too much power and thus endangering the chances for adoption.[38] To this feeling also, may be ascribed the result that, when, later, some urged the insertion of an additional grant "to regulate stages on the post roads," the proposal was not reported from the Committee of Detail.[39] Such a power has, however, been fully exercised.

The report of the Committee of Style, made on September 12, fixed the grant as that "to establish postoffices and postroads," this being the form in which it became a part of the Constitution.[40] Dr. Franklin, however, advocated that there be added "a power to provide for cutting canals where deemed necessary."[41] The motion was seconded, but Mr. Sherman started the opposition by objecting on the ground that the "expense in such cases will fall on the United States and the benefits accrue to the places where the canals may be cut." Mr. Wilson, on the contrary, argued that

---

36 Farrand, vol. i, p. 243.

37 Ibid., vol. ii, p. 177.

38 Ibid., p. 303. New Hampshire, Connecticut, New Jersey, Pennsylvania and North Carolina were opposed. Rhode Island and New York did not vote. The other states were in favor.

39 Ibid., p. 324.

40 Constitution, Art. I, Sec. 8, Clause 7; Farrand, vol. ii, p. 590.

41 Farrand, vol. ii, p. 615.

instead of being an expense to the United States, the canals might be made a source of revenue, and Madison wanted "an enlargement of the motion into a power to grant charters of incorporation where the interest of the United States might require, and the legislative provisions of the individual states might be incompetent. His primary object, however, was to secure an easy communication between the states which the free intercourse, now to be opened, seemed to call for. The political obstacles being removed, a removal of the natural ones as far as possible ought to follow."[42] The question, however, was limited to the single case of canals, and when put to a vote was defeated, because there was an antipathy to monopolies,[43] and because, as Gouverneur Morris admitted, "It was extremely doubtful whether the Constitution they were framing could ever be passed at all by the people of America; that to give it its best chance, however, they should make it as palatable as possible, and put nothing into it, not very essential, which might raise up enemies."[44]

This history of the postal clause in the Federal Convention offers little of interpretative importance. The intent of the framers is sufficiently clear, although, as pointed out by one commentator, the delegation is clothed in words which

---

[42] Farrand, vol. ii, p. 615.

[43] The vote on the motion was 8 to 3 (New Hampshire, Connecticut, Massachusetts, New Jersey, Delaware, Maryland, North Carolina, and South Carolina opposed; Pennsylvania, Virginia, Georgia in favor). This incident in the Federal Convention was to figure in the congressional debates over the incorporation of banks and the construction of postroads. Opinions have differed as to whether the action of the Convention may be said to show that the Constitution did not contemplate the exercise by Congress of a power to incorporate. Madison's record says: "Mr. King thought the power unnecessary. . . . Mr. Wilson mentioned the importance of facilitating by canals the communication with the Western Settlements. As to Banks, he did not think with Mr. King that the power in that point of view would excite the prejudices and parties apprehended. As to mercantile monopolies, they are already included in the power to regulate trade." Farrand, vol. iii, p. 615. Madison's later opinion (1824) was that a general power to incorporate had been negatived. Ibid., p. 463.

[44] Jefferson's Anas in T. J. Randolph, Memoir, Correspondence . . . of Thomas Jefferson, vol. iv, p. 506.

"poorly express its object" and "feebly indicate the particular measures which may be adopted to carry out its design. To establish post offices and post roads is the form of the grant; to create and regulate the entire postal system of the Government is the evident intent."[45]

It is possible partially to explain the specific negativing of the power to cut canals on the ground that there was no limitation to those cases in which the construction would have been an aid to interstate commerce or the transportation of the mails. Under the amendment as proposed Congress would have had the authority to cut a waterway wholly within a state for purely intra-state purposes.[46] As a matter of fact, however, this power, which later was to give rise to considerable controversy, has been exercised by the federal government under its authority to regulate interstate commerce and establish postroads, just as the postal grant itself has been extended to cover fields, neither existing nor within the range of possibility when the Constitution was adopted.

In the state conventions there was practically no discussion of the postal power. Its innocuousness was granted. Mr. Jones of New York was alone in finding a latent aggression, and it was resolved, as the opinion of the state committee, "that the power of Congress to establish post-offices and postroads is not to be construed to extend to the laying out, making, altering, or repairing highways, in any state, without the consent of the legislature of such state."[47] Such a stipulation was destined very soon to become a mere *brutum fulmen.*[48]

---

[45] Pomeroy, Constitutional Law, p. 264.
[46] See Brown, The Commercial Power of Congress, p. 132.
[47] Elliot's Debates, vol. ii, p. 406.
[48] See Moore, American Eloquence, vol. i, p. 349.

CHAPTER II

The Power of Congress to Establish Postoffices

Expansion of Facilities.—"Our whole economic, social and political system," says President Hadley, "has become so dependent upon free and secure postal communication, that the attempt to measure its specific effects can be little less than a waste of words."[1] This is hardly an overstatement of the case, yet, as we have seen, the importance of the postal function was recognized before the Constitution was adopted and when it comprehended only the transmission of intelligence. The increased importance, however, has been absolute as well as relative, since through the postoffice the government now does much more than merely facilitate communication between its citizens.

An act for the temporary establishment of the postoffice was passed by Congress on September 22, 1789.[2] It provided for the appointment of a postmaster general, all the details and regulations to be as they "were under the resolutions and ordinances of the late Congress. The postmaster general to be subject to the direction of the president of the United States, in performing the duties of his office, and in forming contracts for the transportation of the mail."[3]

For a considerable period congressional and administrative efforts were devoted almost exclusively to the extension of facilities; postoffices were established as rapidly as possible; every effort was made to secure speedy transportation of the mail, to insure its security, to prevent private competi-

[1] Art., "Postoffice," Lalor, Cyclopaedia of Political Science, vol. iii, p. 310.

[2] 1 Stat. L. 70.

[3] This act was limited to August 12, 1790. On August 4, 1790, it was continued until March 4, 1791; on March 3 until February 20, 1792, when Congress passed "An Act to establish the postoffice and postroads in the United States." 1 Stat. L. 178, 218, 232.

tion, and by means of an increasingly efficient system to weld together distant parts of the country. The communications of the postmasters general are devoted to recommendations for the improvement of the service;[4] presidential messages take pride in reporting the growth of the establishment, which was rapid. In 1790 there were about 100 postoffices in the country; the receipts from October, 1790 to October, 1791 were $31,706.27 and the disbursements left a balance of $5,498.51.[5]

But in 1823 Monroe was able to report to Congress that 88,600 miles of postroads had been established by law and that the mail was transported over 85,700 miles of this total.[6] During the two years from July 1, 1823 the increase of the transportation of the mail exceeded 1,500,000 miles annually and 1,040 new postoffices were established.[7] In 1828 the total mileage was 114,536 as compared with 5,642 in 1792 and in 1837 was 142,877 miles.[8] The receipts from postage for the year ending March 31, 1828 were $1,058,204.34. These figures serve, in some measure at least, to indicate the rapid expansion of the postal system.[9]

At the same time there was a commensurate recognition of the importance of the establishment in the attitude of Congress and the executive in dealing with it as an administrative arm of the federal government. The act of 1810 referred to the "postoffice establishment"; an incidental use of the word "department" is to be found in the laws of

[4] For example, Gideon Granger, postmaster general, wrote in 1810: "From the nature of our government it becomes a matter of the highest importance to furnish the citizens with full and correct information, and, independent of political considerations, the interests of society will be best promoted, particularly in the interior, by extending to it the facilities of this office. Nor can the seaboard complain as it puts a profit on all that the interior produces for exportation, and on all it consumes from foreign countries." American State Papers (Postoffice), vol. xv, p. 42.

[5] Williams, The American Postoffice, p. 20 (61st Congress, 2d Sess., Sen. Doc. No. 542).

[6] Richardson, Messages and Papers of the Presidents, vol. ii, p. 215.

[7] Ibid., p. 311.

[8] Ibid., p. 419.

[9] Williams, p. 25.

1799 and 1810,[10] but the system became an executive department in 1872 when Congress, codifying the postal laws, passed an act under which the department is now organized.[11] In 1827 the postmaster general's salary was increased to $6,000 per annum, and he was thus placed on an equality with cabinet officers; two years later Jackson made him a member of his official family.[12]

Later in this essay will be found a consideration of the use made by Congress of the postroads clause,[13] in the assumption of authority to aid in works of internal improvement, but here some mention should be made of the connection which has existed between the desire for a speedy transportation of the mail and aid granted to railroads. This aid took the form of donations, with mail service free or at reasonable rates, loans to companies, and general contracts for service, with the purpose of giving aid as well as paying compensation.[14] In debating the desirability of governmental stock subscriptions in transportation undertakings Congress often adverted to the carriage of the mails; and in 1834 it was proposed to give the Baltimore and Ohio Railroad Company $320,000 in return for which the mail was to be carried free forever.[15] Similar suggestions were made from time to time, but there was little definite action, and in 1845 the postmaster general was authorized to contract for the transportation of the mail by railroads, without inviting bids.[16]

Since 1850 the postoffice has not been used, at least

[10] 2 Stat. L. 592, and 1 Stat. L. 733.

[11] Learned, The President's Cabinet, p. 231. See also U. S. v. Kendall, 5 Cranch (U. S. C. C., 1837), 275.

[12] Bassett, Life of Andrew Jackson, vol. ii, p. 413. ". . . in introducing the postmaster general into the cabinet, Jackson began a practice that probably tended, in the long run, to invigorate the workings of the postal establishment, notwithstanding the fact that Barry, successor to McLean in the office, made a conspicuously dismal record." Learned, p. 250.

[13] Below, Chapter III.

[14] See Haney, Congressional History of Railways, p. 319 (Bulletin of the University of Wisconsin: Economic and Political Science Series, vol. iii).

[15] 10 Congressional Debates, 1752.

[16] Haney, p. 323.

avowedly, to aid railways; the period has rather been one of regulation. Disputes have arisen over the proper compensation for service rendered, and companies have refused to give facilities for transportation.[17] It was proposed, therefore, that the roads be forced to carry the mails, and in 1870 an act to this effect was applied in the District of Columbia, compensation to be determined by three commissioners. But in 1872,[18] the codification of the postal laws provided rates for service, with compulsory service by the roads which had received land grants; if the companies were not satisfied with the amounts fixed by Congress, letters were to be forwarded by horse, and the articles for which expedition was not required, were to be sent by stage.[19] At present compensation is determined by an elaborate system, under maximum rates fixed by Congress. The postmaster general may make reductions for refusal to transport, when required, upon the fastest trains,[20] and may impose fines for inefficient service and delays.[21] The necessity has not arisen, but if the railways should refuse to carry the mails, on the ground of inadequate compensation, Congress would have the right to compel transportation, upon reasonable compensation for the taking of private property for public use.[22]

This, however, is only one phase of the financial problem of the postoffice; another, very important phase involves the cost to patrons. Rates for the transmission of letters remained practically unaltered until 1845, while the charges for newspapers were slightly changed in the direction of allowing the publishers special privileges. The act of 1845[23] exercised a broad authority of classification, separat-

[17] 48th Cong., 2d Sess., Sen. Exec. Doc. No. 40.
[18] 16 Stat. L. 115; 17 Stat. L. 309.
[19] Haney, p. 206 (Bulletin of the University of Wisconsin: Economic and Political Science Series, vol. vi).
[20] 23 Stat. L. 156.
[21] See Postal Laws and Regulations of 1913, Title X, "Transportation of the Mails," p. 607 ff.
[22] See 43d Cong., 1st Sess., Sen. Rep. No. 478. This point is developed below, p. 151 ff.
[23] 5 Stat. L. 733.

ing the mail in order to expedite it, and introducing the free privilege for newspapers not more than 1,900 square inches in size, distributed within 30 miles of the place of printing. The act of 1847[24] allowed free exchanges only between publishers, and following this statute many changes were made, both in the conditions of exemption from postage and the rates which were charged. The classification now obtaining was adopted in 1879,[25] and the cent a pound rate for periodical matter admitted to "second class" privileges was fixed in 1885.[26]

But while concessions were made to encourage the circulation of newspapers, Congress maintained rigid restrictions in respect to the size of the packages that could be carried in the mails. The limit was three, and later four pounds. This was originally due to the fact that large packages could not be handled with convenience by the system and were likely to injure or deface other mail matter. But when federal facilities became sufficient to take off, or at least raise, the weight limit, the express companies, which at this time were beginning to derive a large revenue from carrying parcels, were able to postpone congressional action until August 24, 1912[27] when the Parcels Post Act was passed after it had been repeatedly recommended by postmasters general and long desired by public opinion.[28] Such delay has, of course, not been without bitter criticism,[29] and in

---

[24] 9 Stat. L. 202.

[25] 10 Stat. L. 38.

[26] 23 Stat. L. 387. For further details of the special privileges granted periodicals, see Report of the Commission on Second Class Mail Matter (1912), p. 57 ff.

[27] 37 Stat. L. 557. "That hereafter fourth class mail matter shall embrace all other matter, not now embraced by law, in either the first, second, or third class, not exceeding eleven pounds in weight, or greater in size than seventy-two inches in girth and length combined, nor in form or kind likely to injure the person of any postal employee or damage the mail equipment or other mail matter, and not of a character perishable within a period reasonably required for transportation and delivery" (Sec. 8). These limits have been, and will be, raised from time to time.

[28] But see Bodley, "The Post Office Department as a Common Carrier and Bank," 18 American Law Review, 218 (1884).

[29] See Williams, *passim*.

the forties the rise of the express companies, and their transportation of large packets and in some cases of matter which the postoffice undertook to carry, reduced federal revenues and seriously interfered with the efficiency and effectiveness of the government monopoly.[30] But at any time the situation could have been remedied by congressional action. On the other hand, objection has been made to the assumption by Congress under the postoffice clause, of the functions of a common carrier, on the ground that they were not comprehended by the original grant.[31]

Now, Congress clearly has the power to insure, upon the payment of extra fees, the safe transmission of letters or packets to the addressees, but the postal money order system cannot be justified upon any such theory. The act of May 17, 1864[32] authorized the postmaster general to establish, "under such rules and regulations as he may find expedient and necessary, a uniform money order system at all postoffices which he may deem suitable therefor." The law fixed thirty dollars as the maximum amount for which an order could be issued, the purpose of the system being to afford "a cheap, immediate and safe agency for the transfer through the mails of small sums of money."[33] In practice the payee or party for whom the money was intended, was not named in the order, which was given to the applicant upon the payment of the sum specified and the proper fee, and his filling out a printed form of application. This was forwarded to the postmaster at the office upon which the order was drawn, and the latter, therefore, had the information necessary to detect fraud if any was attempted. The

---

[30] Reports of the Postmaster General, 1841–1845.

[31] "It might be easily shown, for instance, that the power over the mails is limited to the transmission of intelligence, and that Congress cannot, consistently with the nature and object of the power, extend it to the ordinary objects of transportation, without a manifest violation of the Constitution, and the assumption of a principle which would give the government control over the general transportation of the country, both by land and water." Speech of John C. Calhoun. 12 Debates of Congress, 1142. See also 18 American Law Review, 218.

[32] 13 Stat. L. 76.

[33] Report of the Postmaster General, 1864, p. 24.

issue of these postal notes was discontinued in 1894,[34] although their use has since been urged;[35] under the money order system as it now obtains, the payee is named in the instrument.[36]

In the Senate there was no debate other than on the administrative features of the law of 1864;[37] the constitutional question was not discussed. Some doubt, however, has since been expressed as to the power of Congress to establish a system of postal savings banks. These were, according to the title of the act, to hold "savings at interest with the security of the government for repayment thereof, and for other purposes." It was provided that available funds should be used in the redemption of United States bonds, and the act recited, "that the faith of the United States is solemnly pledged to the payment of the deposits made in the postal savings depository offices, with accrued interest thereof, as herein provided." This section would seem to imply that the receiving of deposits could be considered as borrowing money on the credit of the United States.

Objection, upon constitutional grounds, was, however, made by Mr. Moon of Tennessee, in a minority report which he presented to the House of Representatives.[38] He argued that no express authority could be found in the Constitution, and that "the depository is not a bank within the legal meaning of that word; nor do the trustees created by this act collect money (deposits) from the people for governmental purposes, but simply become federal trustees of private funds for loan or reinvestment at interest."

It would seem, however, that the provision for redeeming United States bonds and the general tenor of the law, could,

[34] 28 Stat. L. 30.

[35] See Reports of the Postmaster General, 1908–1911.

[36] Postal Laws and Regulations of 1913, Title VIII, "Money Order System," p. 529 ff.

[37] Congressional Globe, 38th Cong., 1st Sess., pp. 1694, 1771, 1861.

[38] Act of June 25, 1910; 36 Stat. L. 814. A system had been recommended by postmasters general in 1871–1873, 1880–1882, 1887–1890, 1907–1909. See 61st Cong., 2d Sess., House Rept. No. 1445, and for Mr. Moon's argument, ibid., Part 2.

without violence, enable the system to be looked upon as established for the purpose of borrowing money on the credit of the United States, or of obviating in some degree the issuance of emergency currency in financial crises through the deposit with the government, and subsequent circulation, of large sums of money which has hitherto been hoarded. But apart from this, while extensions of the postal function to include banking facilities for the receipt of deposits and the issuance of money orders, were certainly not contemplated by the framers of the Constitution, and are not connected with the transmission of intelligence, they are, from foreign precedent, logical parts of the modern postal power. It is extremely difficult, moreover, for a citizen to show an amount of interest sufficient to bring before the courts the constitutionality of such non-essential functions of the government.[39] And especially is this the case when their exercise does not entail taxation, but actually results in increased revenues, and interferes slightly if at all, with the exercise of the same functions by private undertakings. Finally, it should be remembered that the powers granted in the postal clause "are not confined to the instrumentalities of commerce, or the postal service known or in use when the Constitution was adopted, but they keep pace with the progress of the country, and adapt themselves to the new developments of time and circumstances."[40] According to this view there is no constitutional doubt as to the right of the postoffice to engage in the banking activities thus far attempted.

Collectivist Activities.—The primary purpose of the postal power is, of course, the transmission of intelligence, but with vast equipment and organization once in existence, it is a comparatively simple matter for the government to increase in number and in kind, the services which the postoffice may perform for its patrons. In New Zealand postoffices,

[39] Wilson v. Shaw, 204 U. S. 24 (1907).
[40] Pensacola Telegraph Co. v. Western Union Telegraph Co., 96 U. S. 1 (1877).

for example, a person can buy stamps, mail a letter or parcel, send a telegram, deposit money, collect a pension, report births and deaths, and insure his life.[41]

It is due, in part, at least, to the federal system of government in the United States that Congress has been reluctant to increase the functions of the postoffice. But the money order system and postal savings banks have now been established, and it seems inevitable that the telegraph and telephone systems of the country will shortly be nationalized.[42] So also rural free delivery has caused congressional aid to be given to the good roads movement and several schemes have been proposed for extensive road construction under federal auspices.[43]

The inauguration of the parcel post, which in fact has made the postoffice a common carrier, has led to serious efforts on the part of the government towards an adequate appreciation, by possible users, of the advantages of the new facilities, and a campaign of education is carried on, not so much with a view of increasing revenues, as of fostering the "producer to consumer" movement, particularly in farm products. Congress authorized the Secretary of Agriculture "to acquire and diffuse among the people of the United States useful information on subjects connected with the marketing and distributing of farm products" and under this authority the Office of Markets was established on May 16, 1913.[44] It employs specialists in marketing various commodities, and issues bulletins on the facilities for, and advantages of, shipping different products by parcel post. Agents are sent to appropriate sections of the country to do personal work and local offices are active in collecting lists of the names of farmers and others who have produce to

---

41 Davies, The Collectivist State in the Making, p. 39.

42 Below, Chapter VI.

43 Below, p. 80 ff. See also "The States and their Roads," N. Y. Nation, August 20, 1914, and Bourne, "Practical Plan to Spend $3,000,000 for Public Roads," N. Y. Times, May 11, 1913.

44 Annual Reports of the Department of Agriculture, 1914 (Report of the Chief of the Office of Markets).

sell, and printing and distributing these lists to postal patrons who may become purchasers.[45]

It is proposed, furthermore, to use postoffices as employment bureaus, and a bill, the adoption of which was strongly urged on the Sixty-third Congress by Senator Clapp, provided that the postmaster general establish, "under such rules and regulations as he may prescribe, mutual employment exchanges at all presidential postoffices, where registers may be kept of any and all persons who make application to be registered, as either seeking employment, or seeking employees, which information may also be exchanged between such offices, all in the interest of the proper and timely distribution of labor throughout the country."[46] This service would be made self-sustaining through the sale of registration stamps. The bill failed of passage.

But pending action of this character, or the adoption by Congress of legislation designed to lessen unemployment without using the postoffice, the Secretary of Labor and the Postmaster General, cooperated in formulating an arrangement by which "information relating to the distribution of labor could be widely scattered and posted under the auspices of the United States Government.

"The plan," Secretary Wilson goes on to explain, "consists of dated bulletins sent out by the Department of Labor to postmasters throughout the country, by whom they are posted on the bulletin boards so that every postoffice patron, —and this means every man, woman and child,—can easily refer to the information. These are known as 'Bulletins of Opportunities.' They are replaced with others from time to time as necessary, and suitable notice is given when they become inoperative. This plan has received the indorsement of the various state authorities, who have been, and are, cooperating with the Department of Labor in scattering in-

[45] Report of the Postmaster General, 1914, p. 8 ff. See also U. S. Department of Agriculture, Farmers' Bulletins, *inter alia,* Nos. 594 and 611, and The National Parcel Post News (Washington), October 7, 1914, and weekly thereafter.

[46] S. 5180, 63d Cong., 2d Sess. (April 8, 1914).

formation about labor opportunities and conditions in their respective states."[47]

In collectivist facilities, either at present in existence or very seriously urged, the American postoffice is, then, not far behind that of New Zealand. It affords a significant illustration of the tendency of the federal government gradually to engage in many activities, properly national, which are too big for the states, and too expensive or paternalistic for private undertakings. The aim is that the maximum benefit may inure to the citizen.

Postal Crimes.—The postal power, as Marshall pointed out in McCulloch v. Maryland,[48] "is executed by the single act of making the establishment. But from this has been inferred the power and duty of carrying the mail along the postroad, from one postoffice to another. And from this implied power has again been inferred the right to punish those who steal letters from the postoffice, or rob the mail. It may be said with some plausibility that the right to carry the mail and to punish those who rob it is not indispensably necessary to the establishment of a postoffice and postroad. The right is indeed essential to the beneficial exercise of the power, but not indispensably necessary to its existence."

Such a power was asserted even before the adoption of the Constitution; the Ordinance of 1782 meticulously forbade the employees to delay or rob the mails, under penalty of fines "to be used for and recovered in an action of debt" by the treasurer of the United States; a supplementary ordinance attempted to establish a monopoly, and it was made lawful for the postmaster general "to allow and pay to any informer, one moiety of the penalties which may be recovered upon his information, for offences, against the fourth and fifth clauses of the above mentioned ordinance."[49]

The Act of February 20, 1792[50] greatly extended these

---

[47] Wilson, "Uncle Sam; Employment Agent," The Outlook, February 17, 1915, p. 395.
[48] 4 Wheat. 316 (1819).
[49] See above, p. 19.
[50] 1 Stat. L. 232.

criminal provisions, infraction of which was to be punished in the federal courts. Some of the penalties provided for the more serious offences now seem severe, but they are evidence of how important Congress deemed the inviolability of the mails. By this act it was provided, "that if any person shall obstruct or retard the passage of the mail, or of any horse or carriage carrying the same, he shall, upon conviction, for every offence pay a fine not exceeding one hundred dollars. And if any ferryman shall, by wilful negligence, or refusal to transport the mail across any ferry, delay the same, he shall forfeit and pay, for each half hour that the same shall be so delayed, a sum not exceeding ten dollars." A fine and disqualification for holding any office under the United States were the penalties inflicted "if any deputy postmaster or other person authorized by the postmaster general to receive the postage of letters, shall fraudulently demand or receive any rate of postage, or any gratuity or reward, other than is provided by this act for the postage of letters or packets." Vessels were forbidden to enter any port of the United States and break bulk until their letters had been delivered to the postmaster, and the officer of the port could require an oath of delivery. Exception, however, was made in the case of letters to the owner or consignee, and when the vessel had letters directed to another port.

In an effort to make the postal system efficient by insuring it against private competition and the consequent diminution of revenues, there was a provision (still in force, although modified), declaring the federal establishment a monopoly and making any infringement punishable by a fine. The act recited "that if any person, other than the postmaster general or his deputies, or persons by them employed, shall take up, receive, order, dispatch, carry, convey, or deliver, any letter or letters, packet or packets, other than newspapers, for hire or reward, or shall be concerned in setting up any foot or horse post, wagon or other carriage, by or in which any letter or packet shall be carried for hire, on any established postroad, or any packet or other vessel or boat, or any conveyance whatever, whereby the revenue of the general postoffice may be injured, every person so offending shall forfeit for every such offence, the sum of two hundred dollars.[51] *Provided,* that it shall and may be lawful for every person to send letters or packets by special messenger."

Fine and imprisonment were the punishments for unlawfully delaying, embezzling, secreting, or destroying any letter or package not containing money; but if the letter or packet contained any kind of money, negotiable paper, bonds, or warrants, the punishment upon conviction was death. The carrier was forbidden to desert the mail before he reached his destination; robbing any carrier,[52] the mail, or the postoffice was punishable by death. Ten dollars was the penalty for an unlawful use of the franking privilege. One half of all the fines recovered went to the persons informing and prosecuting for the offences, and in 1797 it was provided that accomplices in the commission of postal crimes should be subject to the same punishment as the principals.[53] In 1810 whipping was abolished,[54] but the death penalty for a second robbery, or for putting the carrier's life in jeopardy, was continued. This is strong evidence of congressional insistence upon the sanctity of the mails, since in 1825 only fine and imprisonment were the punishment for assaults on the high seas, or within admiralty jurisdiction with intent to commit a felony.[55]

Upon the basis of these early regulations, Congress has passed many laws calculated to prevent interference with the mails or their misuse; most of the original crimes are still

---

[51] Changed to $50 by the act of May 8, 1794; 1 Stat. L. 354.

[52] Changed by the act of March 2, 1799 (1 Stat. L. 733) to forty lashes and ten years imprisonment for the first offense, but death for the second offense, or if the carrier was wounded or his life put in jeopardy. In 1794 (1 Stat. L. 354) the penalty for stealing mail or letters from the postoffice was changed to fine and imprisonment and in 1799 to thirty lashes and two years imprisonment.

[53] Act of March 3, 1797; 1 Stat. L. 509.

[54] 2 Stat. L. 592.

[55] Act of March 3, 1825; 4 Stat. L. 122.

forbidden and the changes made have been in detail rather than character, with one important exception: there has gradually been built up an *Index Expurgatorius* of articles which it is unlawful to deposit in, or to take from, the mails for purposes of circulation. But with this exception, the penal laws do not differ radically from those of a century ago.

Nearly all "Offenses against the Postal Service" have been brought together as Chapter 8 of the Criminal Code of the United States.[56] It is now unlawful to conduct, or profess to conduct, a postoffice without authority; to carry the mail otherwise than according to law; to set up private expresses; to transport persons unlawfully conveying the mail; to send letters by private express or for carriers to convey them over regular post routes otherwise than in the mail; to wear the uniform of a carrier without authority or to pose as a carrier of the United States mail when such is not in fact the case. Injuring mail bags, stealing postoffice property, stealing or forcing mail locks or keys, breaking into or entering a postoffice, unlawfully entering a postal car, stealing, secreting and embezzling mail matter or its contents,[57] assaulting a carrier with intent to rob and robbing the mail; injuring letter boxes or mail matter; "knowingly and wilfully" obstructing or retarding the passage of the mail, all are crimes punishable in the federal courts.

It is an offence for any employee of the service to detain, destroy or embezzle a letter or newspaper; for a ferryman to "delay the passage of the mail by willful neglect or refusal to transport"; for the master of a vessel to fail to deposit with the postoffice all mail from abroad or to break bulk before making such delivery. No one may sell or use a

---

[56] 35 Stat. L. 1088, 1123.

[57] "Where a letter carrier left a letter in the hall of the residence of the person to whom it was addressed, and the defendant opened it with intent to pry into the business and secrets of the owner" it was held to be a violation of the provision against taking mail before it reached the addressee, and the principle was laid down that the protection extends until the letters reach their destination by actual delivery to the persons entitled to receive them. U. S. v. McCready, 11 Fed. Rep. 225 (1882), citing U. S. v. Hall, 98 U. S. 343 (1878).

cancelled stamp or remove the cancellation marks; postal employees, moreover, are prohibited from making false returns to increase their compensation, from unlawfully collecting postage, from failing to account for postage or to cancel stamps, and from issuing a money order without payment.

There are also, as I have indicated, a number of laws denying the use of the mails for the transmission of obscene or libellous writings, lottery tickets and advertisements, fraudulent matter, poisons, intoxicating liquors, explosives and similar articles which come under the ban of the police power. Furthermore, the complexity of political life and more numerous administrative problems in the service, have given rise to a separate class of offences; thus it is criminal for a member of Congress to be interested in a public contract, or a postal employee in a mail contract; or for an employee to make or receive a political contribution. There is, finally, the so-called "newspaper publicity law," the concluding paragraph of which compels, under penalty of a fine, the marking as an advertisement of all reading matter for the publication of which a valuable consideration is received.[58]

Marshall's *dictum* in McCulloch v. Maryland has remained unquestioned; it has never been doubted that Congress has the power to punish offences against the mails themselves, or neglect of duty by postal employees. The constitutionality of such legislation has never been attacked; the courts have only been called upon to decide technical points. For example, the word "rob" is used in its common law sense; jeopardy "means a well-grounded apprehension of danger to life, in case of refusal or resistance"; pistols are dangerous weapons within the meaning of the law; and "all persons present at the commission of a crime, consenting thereto, aiding, assisting, or abetting therein, or in doing any act which is a constituent of the offence, are principals."[59] The detention of mail by one employed in

[58] Act of August 24, 1912; 37 Stat. L. 554. See below, pp. 121, 164.
[59] U. S. v. Wilson, 1 Baldwin (U. S. C. C.), 78 (1830).

the postoffice, refers to a letter or packet before it reaches its destination; the taking must be clandestine and the intent criminal.[60] An indictment for advising a carrier to rob the mail must aver that the offence has been committed;[61] a sword in the hand, although not drawn, is a dangerous weapon; a pistol is presumed to be charged.[62] These are some of the questions that the courts have been called upon to determine.

Nor has there been any dispute as to the power of Congress to establish a monopoly by forbidding private postal enterprises.[63] As was pointed out in an early case, "No government has ever organized a system of posts without securing to itself, to some extent, a monopoly of the carriage of letters and mailable packets. The policy of such an exclusive system is a subject of legislative, not of judicial inquiry. But the monopoly of the government is an optional, not an essential part of its postal system. The mere existence of a postal department of the government is not an establishment of the monopoly."[64] Thus questions have arisen as to the extent and scope of the original provision and the amendments that have been made to it.

---

60 U. S. v. Pearce, 2 McLean's C. C. R. 14 (1839).

61 U. S. v. Mills, 7 Peters, 138 (1833).

62 U. S. v. Wood, 3 Wash. C. C. R. 440 (1818). See also U. S. v. Hardyman, 13 Peters, 176 (1839).

63 U. S. v. Thompson, 28 Fed. Cas. 97 (1846). But see "The Postoffice Monopoly," 11 Law Reporter, 384 (January, 1849). In this paper the writer argues that the idea of a monopoly is not incidental to the postal grant and that the framers did not intend to make the postoffice a source of general revenue. The Constitution enumerates methods of raising funds and *Expressio unius, exclusio alterius*. Mr. Paterson's plan as proposed to the Convention named the postoffice as a source of revenue, but his language was rejected. May the same, asks this writer, be said of his theory? (p. 396). And if the federal government has no such power it has no right of espionage and it may not say of what "mailable matter" consists (p. 397).

64 U. S. v. Kochersperger, 26 Fed. Cas. 803 (1860). "In a royal grant of the office of postmaster to foreign parts (July 19, 1632, XIX Rymer's Foedera, 385) the monopoly is justified by the consideration 'how much it imports to the state of the King and this realm that the secrets thereof be not disclosed to foreign nations, which cannot be prevented if a promiscuous use of transmitting or taking up of foreign letters and packets should be suffered.'" Freund, Police Power, p. 688, n.

In 1834, for example, New Orleans citizens complained of slow mails, and proposed a plan of forming a private association for a daily express line to New York. But the project being referred to Chancellor Kent for his opinion, he advised that "the objects of the association cannot be carried into effect, in the way proposed, without violating the post-office law."[65] In 1844 the Attorney General gave an opinion that letters carried over mail routes by private carriers could not be charged with postage, nor could the letters be detained; the only available course was "to enforce the penalties to which all unauthorized carriers of letters on the mail routes are by law subjected."[66]

As for the general interpretation of the statute, a federal circuit court, in holding that it was not unlawful to carry an unstamped letter of advice concerning money shipped by express, said: "These provisions of the postoffice law, being in derogation of common right, must be construed strictly, and in the absence of clear and explicit language, forbidding the carriage of a letter, under the circumstances indicated, we must hold that the right to do so is not interfered with."[67] The Supreme Court of the United States, however, had previously declared that the act was undoubtedly a revenue law,[68] although "not drawn with all the precision and explicitness desirable in penal legislation." And the rule of interpretation as laid down by the Department of Justice was that the acts "are not subjected to the narrow rules formerly applied in the construction of penal statutes. . . . In our courts, such acts receive the same construction that

[65] Act of March 2, 1827; 4 Stat. L. 238; Niles' Register, vol. xlvii, p. 120. Until 1827 newspapers could be carried privately, but by the act of this year an express exception hitherto existing was omitted. At the present time, of course, they may be carried outside of the mail. See Postal Laws and Regulations of 1913, p. 605.

[66] 4 Opinions of the Attorneys General, 349 (1844). If a passenger takes the letters without the knowledge of the carrier, the latter is not liable and no penalty is incurred by the person sending the letters; but if the practice is known by public advertisement the carrier will be liable and also the person employing agents to carry his mail. U. S. v. Hall, 26 Fed. Cas. 75 (1844).

[67] U. S. v. U. S. Express Co., 5 Biss. 91 (1869).

[68] U. S. v. Bromley, 12 How. 88 (1851). See also 4 Ops. 159 (1843).

would be put upon any other remedial legislation; that is, a fair, sensible, practical interpretation, without reference to any merely technical rule in favor of the accused."[69]

The question arose in 1858 as to the legality of carrying letters to and from the postoffice in a town where a public carrier had not been appointed. The attorney general was of the opinion that the act forbade this. "A person," he said, "who intends to make the carrying of letters his regular business, or part of his business, and to do it periodically for hire, in opposition to the public carrier, is legally incapable of receiving authority to take letters out of the postoffice for that purpose."[70] But when the question went to the courts, a contrary position was taken. The Act of March 3, 1851[71] authorized the postmaster general "to establish postroutes within the cities or towns." The court held that the word "postroutes" was not synonymous with "postroads" used in that portion of the act of 1827 which made criminal attempts to compete with the federal government in carrying the mail. Hence private letter carriers violated no law. This decision,[72] however, was overruled when Congress extended[73] the provisions of the Act of 1827 to all postroutes already, or thereafter established, and in 1872[74] declared letter carrier routes within cities "postroads."[75]

---

69 4 Ops. 162. "By the now settled doctrine of this court" revenue statutes are "not to be construed like penal laws generally, strictly in favor of the defendant; but they are to be fairly and reasonably construed, so as to carry out the intention of the legislature." U. S. v. Stowell, 133 U. S. 1 (1890).

70 9 Ops. 161 (1858); but see U. S. v. Kochersperger, above.

71 9 Stat. L. 591.

72 U. S. v. Kochersperger, above. While resting its decision on a literal interpretation of the statute, the court intimated that the public streets of a municipality were different from highways, and expressed doubt as to whether they could "be established by Congress as postroads for any other purpose than the carriage of the mail." See below, p. 151.

73 Act of March 2, 1861; 12 Stat. L. 205.

74 Act of June 8, 1872; 17 Stat. L. 309.

75 Blackham v. Gresham, 16 Fed. Rep. 609 (1883). In 1872, citizens of Davenport, Iowa, were permitted to employ a private dispatch company to deliver within the city limits mail upon which no U. S. postage had been paid; this was allowed because the streets of the city had not been made postroutes. 14 Ops. 152.

Thus when an express company had a number of messengers to collect letters daily from certain customers who paid with private stamps, previously sold, the letters being taken to an office, sorted, and dispatched to the addressees, the court held that these deliveries could not be deemed "by messenger employed for the particular occasion only," but were deliveries "by regular trips and at stated periods," and the defendant was therefore liable.[76]

There has always been the exception that the carrier is permitted to transport, otherwise than in the mail, letters or packets relating "to some part of the cargo of such steamboat or other vessel, *to the current business of the carrier,* or to some article" carried at the same time.[77] Under this inhibition it is not lawful for a railroad company to carry letters from one connecting line to another line, when the letters relate to through business. The letters must be sent by, or addressed to, the carrying company.[78] But in 1912 Attorney General Wickersham decided that a railroad might carry over its lines, not in the mail, letters written by the secretary of a relief association (which was composed of the employees of the railroad) to the railroad company, but not letters from the officers of the association to its members.[79]

In 1915 the Supreme Court was called upon to construe the statute and held within the "current business" exception "letters of a telegraph superintendent, jointly appointed and paid by a railway company, and a telegraph company, which were written to a railway station agent and telegraph operator with the purpose of promoting the efficient and successful operation of the telegraph business in the success of which the railway company, under the contract with the telegraph company, has a financial interest." The Court refused, however, to consider whether the statute is "penal

---

[76] U. S. v. Easson, 18 Fed. Rep. 590 (1883).

[77] Rev. Stat. Sec. 3985; the italicised words were added by the Act of March 4, 1909; 35 Stat. L. 1124. See 21 Ops. 394 (1896); 28 Ops. 537 (1910), and 42 Cong. Rec., 973 ff.

[78] 21 Ops. 394.

[79] 29 Ops. 418 (1912).

or remedial, or whether it is to have a strict or a liberal interpretation."[80]

Another class of offences has arisen out of the section providing punishment for "whoever shall knowingly and wilfully obstruct or retard the passage of the mail," or any conveyance by which it is being carried. Wide extension of federal authority and effective federal supremacy have been enforced under this provision, it having been held that a defendant toll gate keeper cannot plead the justification of a state law for stopping a carrier of the mail.[81] It has been decided, also, that mail matter in the postoffice, ready for delivery, is "obstructed" within the meaning of the statute by an unprovoked assault on the postmaster. "The law presumes that the defendant intended by his act the result which followed and the offense is complete." An act, if unlawful, resulting in an obstruction, is *per se* done knowingly and wilfully.[82]

Preventing a mail train from running as made up, even though one is willing that the mail car shall go on, is an obstruction within the meaning of the statute,[83] and where the regular passenger trains of a railroad company have been selected as the ones to carry the mail, the failure of the railroad to run other trains for that purpose is not necessarily unlawful.[84] It is no defense, however, that the obstruction was effected merely by leaving the employment,

---

[80] U. S. v. Erie R. Co., 235 U. S. 513 (1915). It was held that the setting up of a post by a railroad car or steamboat was not within the act of 1827. "Since the passing of the postoffice laws new modes of conveyance have been established and a condition of things arisen not then known or contemplated. And the question is, whether new acts in contravention of the general spirit and policy of the laws, can be brought within any of its prohibitions, and subjected to a specific penalty. However willing the court might be to attain that end, it cannot strain or force the language used beyond its fair and usual meaning." U. S. v. Kimball, 26 Fed. Cas. 782 (1844).

[81] U. S. v. Sears, 55 Fed. Rep. 268 (1893).

[82] U. S. v. Claypool, 14 Fed. Rep. 127 (1882).

[83] U. S. v. Clark, 25 Fed. Cas. 443 (1877); see also In Re Grand Jury, 62 Fed. Rep. 840 (1894).

[84] In Re Grand Jury, 62 Fed. Rep. 834 (1894).

"where the motive of quitting was to retard the mails, and had nothing to do with the terms of employment."[85]

These doctrines were given their widest scope in the Debs cases. It was held that an indictment for obstructing the mails need not set out that the act was done feloniously, since the crime was not a felony at the common law; nor, furthermore, is it necessary to show knowledge that the mails would be interfered with. "The laws make all railways postroutes of the United States," said the court, "and it is within the range of everyone's knowledge that a large proportion of the passenger trains on these roads carry the mails." Finally where the indictment is for conspiracy to obstruct the mails, and overt acts in pursuance thereof, "it is not restricted to a single overt act, since the gist of the offense is conspiracy, which is a single offense."[86]

The authority of Congress may, moreover, be enforced otherwise than by prosecution for violations of this provision. "The entire strength of the nation," said the Supreme Court, "may be used to enforce in any part of the land the full and free exercise of all national powers and the security of all rights entrusted by the Constitution to its care. The strong arm of the national government may be put forth to brush away all obstructions to the freedom of interstate commerce or the transportation of the mails. If the emergency arises the army of the Nation, and all its militia, are at the service of the Nation to compel obedience to its laws." And the Supreme Court went on to declare that "it is equally within its [the federal government's] competency to appeal to the civil courts for an inquiry and determination as to the existence and character of any alleged obstructions, and if such are found to exist, or threaten to occur, to invoke the powers of those courts to remove or restrain such obstructions; that the jurisdiction of the courts to interfere in such matters by injunction is one recognized from ancient times and by indubitable authority; . . . that the proceeding by

[85] Thomas v. Cincinnati, etc., Ry. Co., 62 Fed. Rep. 803 (1894); but see U. S. v. Stevens, 27 Fed. Cas. 1312 (1877).

[86] U. S. v. Debs, 65 Fed. Rep. 210 (1895).

injunction is of a civil character and may be enforced by proceedings in contempt; that such proceedings are not in execution of the criminal laws of the land; that the penalty for a violation of the injunction is no substitute for and no defence to a prosecution for any criminal offences committed in the course of such violation."[87]

When we turn, however, to the power of Congress to exclude from the mails, a different problem is presented. As has been pointed out, early in the history of the postoffice, mail matter was classified according to its character and different rates of postage were charged. In 1799 the Postmaster General sent a letter to Congress complaining of "large and inconvenient packages" and the Act of 1810 provided that "no postmaster shall be obliged to receive, to be conveyed by mail, any packet which shall weigh more than three pounds."[88] Congress, therefore, very early exercised the right of determining what articles should be mailable and the conditions upon which they should be carried.

These exclusions were made to protect the mails. Objection was made to the "inconvenient packages" on the ground that the transit was retarded and smaller articles were injured. Such restrictions have been maintained, the postoffice regulations now prescribing the limits, both of weight and size. Congress has, moreover, on the same ground, conditionally excluded a variety of articles, such as poisons, explosives, inflammable materials, infernal machines, disease germs, and all compositions liable to hurt anyone or injure the mails. It is provided, however, that the postmaster general "may permit the transmission in the mails under such rules and regulations as he shall prescribe as to preparation and packing" of any of these articles, "not outwardly or of their own force dangerous or injurious to life, health and property." Intoxicating liquors are absolutely excluded. Any violations of the statutory

---

[87] In Re Debs, 158 U. S. 564 (1895). See also Fairlie, National Administration, p. 38; Cleveland, The Government in the Chicago Strike, *passim*, and 23 McClure's Magazine, p. 227.

[88] 2 Stat. L. 592.

provisions or of regulations made by the postmaster general in pursuance of the authority given him, are punishable by fine and imprisonment.[89]

The absolute exclusion of intoxicants, however, cannot be justified upon the same principles as the conditional exclusions, since the danger to the mails can only arise from the fact that they are liquids. This distinction leads naturally to another class of articles which are denied postal facilities on account of the effect they will have on recipients. In this class is all printed or written matter which is obscene, libellous and indecent, or which relates to lotteries and fraudulent schemes.[90]

The first inhibition was made by Congress in the Act of March 3, 1865, and by the Act of June 8, 1872, codifying previous laws and organizing the postoffice on its present basis, the use of the mails was denied to obscene matter, cards "upon which scurrilous epithets may have been written or printed, or disloyal devices printed or engraved" and "letters or circulars concerning illegal lotteries."[91] It has since been made criminal to take obscene or scurrilous matter from the mails for purposes of circulation.[92]

Before the Supreme Court of the United States, the power of Congress to exclude obscene and indecent matter from the mails[93] has never been seriously questioned, and the points presented for determination, largely to the lower federal courts, have not been as to the constitutional author-

---

[89] 35 Stat. L. 1131. See Postal Laws and Regulations of 1913, p. 255.

[90] Publications which violate copyrights granted by the United States cannot be mailed. In this case the postal power is used to make more effectual legislation which it was competent for Congress to enact. See Postal Laws and Regulations of 1913, p. 264.

[91] 13 Stat. L. 507; 17 Stat. L. 283, 302.

[92] Postal Laws and Regulations of 1913, p. 264.

[93] As to when one, who does not personally mail non-mailable matter, may be regarded as causing it to be deposited in the mails, see Demolli v. U. S., 144 Fed. Rep. 363 (1906); 6 L. R. A. n. s. 424, and note. Importation into the United States of obscene matter or articles of an immoral nature was forbidden by the act of March 2, 1857, 11 Stat. L. 168.

ity of Congress.[94] In 1890, the Supreme Court held that under the Act of July 12, 1876 it was not an offence to deposit in the mails an obscene letter, enclosed in an envelope, and refused to consider the amendment made in 1888 which had extended the inhibition to sealed matter, closed to inspection.[95] But in 1895, the Court determined that while the possession of obscene pictures is not forbidden, it is an offence to deposit in the mails a letter, not in itself objectionable, but conveying information as to where, and of whom, such pictures could be obtained.[96] And the next year the Court refused to accept the defence that the obscene matter was mailed in reply to decoy letters by a government detective.[97]

It was held, moreover, that "the words 'obscene,' 'lewd' and 'lascivious,' as used in the statute, signify that form of immorality which has relation to sexual impurity, and have the same meaning as is given them at common law in prosecutions for obscene libel. As the statute is highly penal, it should not be held to embrace language unless it is fairly within its letter and spirit."[98] The penal code of

---

[94] "For more than thirty years, not only has the transmission of obscene matter been prohibited, but it has been made a crime, punishable by fine or imprisonment, for a person to deposit such matter in the mails. The constitutionality of this law, we believe, has never been attacked." Public Clearing House v. Coyne, 194 U. S. 497 (1904), but see Dunlop v. U. S., 165 U. S. 486 (1897), and U. S. v. Popper, 98 Fed. Rep. 423 (1899).

[95] U. S. v. Chase, 135 U. S. 255 (1890). The statute applied to any "book, pamphlet, picture, writing, print, or other publication" of an obscene character. R. S. sec. 3893. The prosecution in the Chase case arose before the act of September 26, 1888, which the Court refused to consider, and which extended the inhibition to sealed letters. 25 Stat. L. 496.

[96] Grimm v. U. S., 156 U. S. 604 (1895). The Chase case was followed by U. S. v. Wilson, 58 Fed. Rep. 768 (1893), which held that even under the act of 1888 "or other publication" were qualifying words which excluded letters, and by U. S. v. Warner, 59 Fed. Rep. 355 (1894); *contra,* U. S. v. Nathan, 61 Fed. Rep. 936 (1894), and U. S. v. Ling, 61 Fed. Rep. 1001 (1894). All doubt was removed by Grimm v. U. S.

[97] Andrews v. U. S., 162 U. S. 420 (1896).

[98] Swearingen v. U. S., 161 U. S. 446 (1896), Justices Harlan, Gray, Brown and White dissenting, followed in U. S. v. Moore, 104 Fed. Rep. 78 (1900); U. S. v. O'Donnell, 165 Fed. Rep. 218 (1908); U. S. v. Benedict, 165 Fed. Rep. 221 (1908), and Knowles v. U. S., 170 Fed. Rep. 409 (1909).

1909 extended the language to exclude "every filthy" book, pamphlet, picture or letter, and this in effect overruled the Swearingen case.[99]

There have been questions, also, as to the requirements for a valid indictment, which, it has been held, need not set out the objectionable matter, but must inform the accused of the nature of the charge against him.[100] The courts have varied as to whether the test of obscenity is that laid down by Lord Cockburn: Is the tendency of the matter "to deprave and corrupt those whose minds are open to such immoral influences and into whose hands a publication of this sort would fall"?[101] or the dictionary meaning as "offensive to chastity, decency or delicacy." The question as to what is obscene, however, is for the jury to determine.[102]

Congress has also denied postal facilities to "all matter otherwise mailable by law, upon the envelope or outside cover or wrapper of which, or any postal card upon which any delineations, epithets, terms, or language of an indecent, lewd . . . libelous, scurrilous, defamatory, or threatening character, or calculated by the terms or manner or style of display and obviously intended to reflect injuriously upon the character or conduct of another, may be written or printed or otherwise impressed or apparent." This prohibition has been extended to include a postal card demanding the payment of a debt and stating that "if it is not paid at once we shall place the same with our lawyer for collection."[103]

It has been held, however, that "outside cover or wrapper" does not include the outside sheet of a newspaper

---

[99] U. S. v. Dempsey, 185 Fed. Rep. 450 (1911). See also, "Exclusion of Certain Publications from the Mails," Hearing before Committee on the Postoffice and Postroads, House of Representatives, February 1, 1915, p. 6. But the postmaster general in his Annual Report of 1914, p. 47, appears to think that the Swearingen case is still controlling.

[100] Rosen v. U. S., 161 U. S. 29 (1896).

[101] Reg. v. Hicklin, L. R. 3, Q. B. 360 (1868).

[102] Knowles v. U. S., 170 Fed. Rep. 409 (1909); U. S. v. Bennett, 16 Blatch. 343 (1879), and U. S. v. Kennerley, 209 Fed. Rep. 119 (1913).

[103] U. S. v. Boyle, 40 Fed. Rep. 664 (1889).

and thus the postal authorities are unable to exclude periodical publications on the ground that they contain scurrilous or defamatory matter.[104] From time to time bills have been introduced in Congress to authorize the postmaster general to exclude from the second-class privilege publications, as such, single issues of which are found to contain such non-mailable matter; but no favorable action has ever been taken by Congress on any of these bills. An effort has also been made to deny all postal facilities in such cases.[105]

Vigorous objection has been made to the validity of laws excluding obscene matter, but the arguments have in no case any authoritative sponsorship. One writer, for example, urges that "under the pretext of regulating the mails," Congress controls "the psycho-sexual condition of the postal patrons." "The statute," he goes on to say, "furnishes no standard or test by which to differentiate what book is obscene from that which is not."[106] Such a contention, so far as it is one of *constitutional weakness* in Congress is plainly invalid. Immoral libels are an offence at the common law, "not because it is either the duty or province of the law to promote religion or morality by any direct means or punishments, but because the line which must be drawn is between what is and is not the average tone of morality

[104] Postmaster General Blair in 1861 excluded from the mails twelve treasonable publications, "of which several had been previously presented by the grand jury as incendiary and hostile to constitutional authority." Report of the Postmaster General, 1861, p. 584. In 1914 the postmaster at Greenville, Pa., threw out of the mail several thousand cards containing facsimile appeals over his signature by Colonel Roosevelt, calling upon all good citizens to oppose Senator Boies Penrose. The local postmaster held the cards to be defamatory, but his decision was reversed by the authorities at Washington. See N. Y. Sun, October 31, 1914.

[105] See below, p. 158 ff.

[106] Schroeder, Free Press Anthology, p. 171. See also his "Obscene" Literature and Constitutional Law. In The Unanswered Argument against the Constitutionality of the so-called Comstock Postal Laws, and for the Inviolability and Free and Equal Use of the United States Mail, T. B. Wakeman argues that Congress has no legislative power over the subject, and that "the power to suppress obscenity and indecency, together with all other crimes or offenses is one of the general powers reserved in the United States Constitution to the people and the states," p. 30.

which each person is entitled to expect at the hands of his neighbor as the basis of their mutual dealings."[107] The standard to determine what is obscene is the same as that which has prevailed at the common law.

The right of individuals to use the mails is not an absolute one; the legislative department of the government may impose reasonable restrictions on its exercise. It may say that a public convenience is not to be used to injure the morals of the citizens and may exclude such injurious matter, not with the view of making immorality criminal, but simply in order that the circulation may not be encouraged by the government. And to make this denial of facilities effective, Congress may punish violations. The grant of the postal power (to borrow the language used by the Supreme Court in a commerce case) "is complete in itself," and "Congress, as an incident to it, may adopt not only means necessary but convenient to its exercise, and the means may have the quality of police regulations." The right to use the mails is "given for beneficial exercise," and may be denied when it "is attempted to be perverted to and justify baneful existence."[108]

With regard to lotteries, however, the case is not so clear. The law declared that "no letter or circular concerning [illegal] lotteries, so-called gift concerts, or other similar enterprises, offering prizes, or concerning schemes devised and intended to deceive and defraud the public, for the purpose of obtaining money under false pretenses, shall be carried in the mail," and made violation criminal.[109] In 1876 the word "illegal" was stricken out, so that letters or circulars concerning all lotteries were prohibited,[110] and in 1890 the law was further amended so as to include lottery advertisements in newspapers and to permit postmasters to withhold suspected mail.[111] Trial of offenders may take

[107] Patterson, Liberty of the Press, and Public Worship, p. 69.

[108] Hoke v. U. S., 227 U. S. 308 (1913). See "Is Congress a Conservator of the Public Morals?", 38 American Law Review, 194.

[109] R. S. sec. 3894.

[110] 19 Stat. L. 90.

[111] 26 Stat. L. 465; see also 16 Ops. 5 (1878).

place either in the district where the letter was mailed, or that to which it was addressed.[112]

The Senate Committee in charge of the amendments proposed in 1890, reported the bill to be based "on the conceded power of the government to determine what character of matter may be sent through the mails; and its purpose is to protect the general welfare and morality of the people against the pernicious effects of lotteries."[113] For authority the committee relied upon the case of Phalen v. Virginia, in which the Supreme Court said:

"The suppression of nuisances injurious to public health or morality is among the most important duties of government. Experience has shown that the common forms of gambling are comparatively innocuous when placed in contrast with the widespread pestilence of lotteries. The former are confined to a few persons and places, but the latter infests the whole community: it enters every dwelling; it reaches every class; it preys upon the hard earnings of the poor; it plunders the ignorant and simple." At common law, the committee argued, the king could not sanction a nuisance; by parity of reasoning a nuisance may be denied governmental encouragement.[114]

All of the anti-lottery legislation, enacted by Congress, has been sustained by the Supreme Court of the United States, although, I think, the reasoning might well have been more cogent. In the first case arising under the earlier legislation, the Court declared:

"The validity of legislation prescribing what should be carried, and its weight and form and the charges to which it should be subjected, has never been questioned. . . . The power possessed by Congress embraces the regulation of

[112] R. S. sec. 731, and Palliser v. U. S., 136 U. S. 257 (1890). This was a case where a letter was mailed in New York and addressed to a postmaster in Connecticut to induce him to violate his official duty. The District Court for the district of Connecticut was declared to have jurisdiction.

[113] 51st Cong., 1st Sess., Sen. Rep. No. 1579; see also House Rep. No. 2844.

[114] 8 Howard, 164 (1850).

the entire postal system of the country. The right to designate what shall be carried necessarily involves the right to determine what shall be excluded."[115] And in a later case, under the act of 1890, the freedom of the press also being at issue, the Court said:

"The states before the Union was formed could establish postoffices and postroads and in doing so could bring into play the police power in the protection of their citizens from the use of the means so provided for purposes supposed to exert a demoralizing influence upon the people. When the power to establish postoffices and postroads was surrendered to the Congress it was as a complete power, and the grant carried with it the right to exercise all the powers which made that power effective. It is not necessary that Congress should have the power to deal with crime and immorality within the states in order to maintain that it possesses the power to forbid the use of the mails in aid of the perpetration of crime and immorality."[116]

Counsel for the petitioners in this case urged with considerable force that there was a valid distinction between obscene or indecent matter and lottery tickets and advertisements, but to this the Court replied:

"The argument that there is a distinction between *mala prohibita* and *mala in se,* and that Congress might forbid the use of the mails in promotion of such acts as are universally regarded as *mala in se,* including all such crimes as murder, arson, burglary, etc., and the offence of circulating obscene books and papers, but cannot do so in respect of other matters which it might regard as criminal or immoral, but which it has no power itself to prohibit, involves a concession which is fatal to the contention of the petitioners, since it would be for Congress to determine what are within and what are without the rule; but we think there is no room for such a distinction here, and that it must be left to Congress in the exercise of a sound discretion to determine in

[115] Ex parte Jackson, 96 U. S. 727 (1878).
[116] In Re Rapier, 143 U. S. 110 (1892).

what manner it will exercise the power which it undoubtedly possesses."

Special exception is taken by Mr. Hannis Taylor to the doctrines of the Rapier case. He says: "The act against the circulation of immoral literature, which was not drawn in a paroxysm of excitement, exhausts the entire constitutional authority over the intellectual contents of documents passing through the mails that Congress can exercise." And referring to the exclusion of lottery tickets and advertisements: "This new born heresy—created to meet a special emergency—will be utterly repudiated by the American people the moment when the despotic and irresponsible power over opinion with which the fiat of the Supreme Court has armed Congress, is applied, as it surely will be, to some subject which will arouse and quicken the public conscience."[117]

As yet, however, there has been manifested no disposition to repeal any of the lottery legislation. Congress has, in fact, made further exclusions, with slight popular protest. The act of July 31, 1912, excludes from interstate commerce, from the mails, and from importation into the United States, "any film or other pictorial representation or encounter of pugilists, under whatever name, which is designed to be used or may be used for purposes of public exhibition."[118] This, probably, is the most advanced action yet taken by Congress.

It should be noticed, however, in concluding this review, that all articles which Congress has thus far excluded from the mails have been inherently different from the articles which may be transmitted, in that they may have a harmful effect on other mail or on recipients. Explosives, liquids, infernal machines, intoxicating liquors,—all are in their nature dangerous to the mail or to the addressees. Obscene literature and lottery tickets are proper subjects for denuncia-

---

117 "A Blow at the Freedom of the Press," in 155 North American Review, p. 694.

118 Act of July 31, 1912; 37 Stat. L. 240. But see Keller v. U. S., 213 U. S. 138 (1908).

tion by the government and Congress may attempt to minimize their evil by denying them postal facilities. It may be said, therefore, that all prohibitory legislation has had the character of police regulations; each exclusion, when assailed, has been justified on the facts of the particular case, and the Supreme Court has never gone so far as has a lower federal tribunal in declaring that, "Congress has exclusive jurisdiction over the mails and may prohibit the use of the mails for the transmission of any article. Any article, of any description, whether harmless or not, may, therefore, be declared contraband in the mail by act of Congress and its deposit there made a crime."[119]

Fraud Orders.—The denial of postal privileges when they are used to defraud may be justified upon the same grounds as the exclusion of obscene matter and lottery tickets; Congress has authority to make the use of the mails subject to police regulations. But it is provided that "the postmaster general may, upon evidence satisfactory to him that any person or company is engaged in conducting any lottery"[120] or fraudulent scheme, "instruct postmasters at any post-office at which registered letters arrive directed to any such person or company . . . to return all such registered letters to the postmaster at the office at which they were originally mailed, with the word 'Fraudulent' plainly written or stamped upon the outside thereof" and they may be returned to the writers under such regulations as the postmaster general may prescribe. But under this section there is no authority to open any sealed letter.[121]

The constitutionality of these provisions has been fully established by the Supreme Court of the United States, which has held that the postal system is not "a necessary part of the civil government in the same sense in which the protection of life, liberty and property, the defense of the

---

[119] U. S. v. Bott, 24 Fed. Cas. 1204 (1873).

[120] As to what constitutes a lottery see Eastman v. Armstrong Byrd Music Co., 212 Fed. Rep. 662 (1914); 52 L. R. A. n. s. 108, and note.

[121] Postal Laws and Regulations of 1913, p. 267.

government against insurrection, and foreign invasion and the administration of public justice are; but it is a public function, assumed and established by Congress for the general welfare." Thus it was constitutional to exclude such fraudulent matter.

As to other objections, the Court declared that due process of law was not denied when an executive official was given authority to control the disposition of property; "nor do we think the law unconstitutional because the postmaster general may seize and detain all letters, which may include letters of a purely personal or domestic character, and having no connection whatever with the prohibited enterprise." The fact that the postmaster general may not open letters not addressed to himself makes such a provision necessary in order that the law may be effective. Finally, said the Court, "the objection that the postmaster general is authorized by statute to confiscate the money, or the representative of the money, of the addressee, is based upon the hypothesis that the money or other article of value contained in a registered letter becomes the property of the addressee as soon as the letter is deposited in the postoffice." But the postmaster general, in seizing the letter, does not confiscate it, or change title thereto; he merely denies the use of the facilities of the postoffice. It would be proper for Congress to empower the postmaster general, in the first instance, to refuse to receive the letter at all, if its objectionable character is known to him.[122]

The sole remaining question is therefore as to the conclusiveness of administrative determinations and it appears that in the postoffice cases the courts have exercised their powers of review further than in any others coming up from different executive departments.[123] The Supreme Court has summarized the rule as follows: "That where the decision of

---

122 Public Clearing House v. Coyne, 194 U. S. 497 (1904).

123 See Brinton, "Some Powers and Problems of the Federal Administrative," University of Pennsylvania Law Review, January, 1913, reprinted as 62d Cong., 3d Sess., Sen Doc. No. 1054. See also Pierce, Federal Usurpation, p. 335 ff.

questions of fact is committed by Congress to the judgment and discretion of the head of a department, his decision thereon is conclusive; and that even upon mixed questions of law and fact, or of law alone, his action will carry with it a strong presumption of its correctness and the courts will not ordinarily review it, although they may have the power and will occasionally exercise the right of so doing."[124]

But it is necessary that the facts upon which the administrative decision is based be not such that the application of the statute will be a clear mistake of law. Thus, in American Magnetic School of Healing v. McAnnulty, the postmaster general in effect made a fraud order depend on his opinion as to the efficacy of the complainant's method of healing by encouraging the proper use of the mind to correct physical ailments. The court ruled that under no construction was there evidence sufficient to show fraud. "To authorize the interference of the postmaster general," said the decision, "the facts stated must, in some aspect, be sufficient to permit him, under the statutes, to make the order."[125] Or, expressed differently, if it is "legally impossible" under any interpretation of the facts, "to hold that the complaining party was engaged in obtaining money through the mails by false or fraudulent representations," the courts will intervene.[126] The general rule may, therefore, be stated as follows: Judicial review will be granted only in those cases where it appears that the order is without legal authority; exercise of discretion will not be reviewed unless, upon any construction of the facts, the order is clearly wrong, and even upon questions of law alone, it will carry a strong presumption of correctness.

A number of proposals have been made and bills introduced in Congress to provide for a judicial review of the postmaster general's decisions. Congressman Crumpacker,

---

124 Bates & Guild Co. v. Payne, 194 U. S. 106 (1904).

125 American School of Magnetic Healing v. McAnnulty, 187 U. S. 94 (1902).

126 Missouri Drug Co. v. Wyman, 129 Fed. Rep. 623 (1904). See also U. S. ex rel. Reinach v. Cortelyou, 28 App. D. C. 570 (1906), 12 L. R. A. n. s. 166, and note.

for instance, argued "that in all departments of government there is no instance where substantial rights are taken from a citizen upon confidential reports without a legal right to be heard and to see and examine the evidence that is submitted against him, aside from the fraud order and practice in the postoffice department."[127] He urged that the law should be changed and a copy of the order served on the concern suspected of fraudulent practices. This order should not become operative for fifteen days, except to the extent of holding the mail undelivered in the postoffice. The aggrieved party could file a bill in the circuit court with a bond of $500 and a summary trial at law would be held upon the issue, which the court should formulate upon the facts involved. Appeal would lie and pending final action the mail would be held in the postoffice or disposed of by order of the court. Another bill authorized a review after the orders had been issued.

Vigorous objection to such changes in the law was made by the postoffice authorities. A memorandum filed by the assistant attorney general for the department[128] declared that the prime object of the regulations was to secure summary action. "The value of the law depends upon the promptness with which schemes to defraud may be denied the use of the mails to further the swindle. If action is delayed any considerable time,—as would necessarily be the case in a judicial proceeding,—the scheme will consummate its fraud before the interference occurs." If Mr. Crumpacker's bill became law, the only effectual action would be criminal prosecution, and this is always difficult since the victimized parties live at a distance, and it is hard to get evidence to offer at the trial.

In practice, the memorandum explained, investigations are made by inspectors of cases where fraudulent practices are

127 Statement of Hon. E. D. Crumpacker before the House of Representatives Committee on the Judiciary, May 25, 1906, in support of H. R. 16548.

128 Memorandum by the Assistant Attorney General for the Postoffice Department on Postal "Fraud Order" Law (1906).

alleged, and reports sent to the department. If a *prima facie* case of fraud is established, the person or concern involved is notified and given an opportunity to appear before the assistant attorney general for the postoffice department; after the hearing a report is made to the postmaster general who takes final action. But such a hearing is not required by the statute.[129]

The codification of postal laws presented to Congress in 1908, provided for the creation of a Commission of Postal Appeals, to consist of three members, one of whom must be a lawyer, appointed by the President. One of its duties would be to "pass upon the issuance of fraud orders against persons alleged to be conducting lotteries, gift enterprises, or schemes to defraud." Cases would be submitted by the assistant attorney general upon his being satisfied that the evidence was legally sufficient to justify the order which the Commission would issue or refuse after a hearing; provisional action, however, could be taken, and pending final determination, the mail matter could be held in the postoffice.[130]

[129] "It must also be borne in mind that the idea of the fraud order law is not punitive, but is simply protective. It is to prevent the use of the mails to defraud the public. The theory is that by the stopping of the mail privileges in the initiating stages of the fraud, the consummation of the scheme will be prevented. It would be utterly impossible to fulfill this purpose by a trial in court, for the necessary legal evidence could not generally be obtained until the scheme had run its course." Ibid., p. 6.

[130] Final Report of the Joint Commission on the Business Method of the Postoffice Department and the Postal Service (December 17, 1908), 60th Cong., 2d Sess., Sen. Rep. No. 701, chap. 4, secs. 90–99.

CHAPTER III

The Power of Congress to Establish Postroads

Legislative Action.—Apart from the postoffice, problems of road construction and internal improvements, by the necessities of development, almost immediately confronted the new nation, which scanned the delegated powers in the Federal Constitution, and not finding any specific authorization of congressional action, asserted the right upon several clauses, among them being the one to establish postroads. By 1793 there were only one hundred and ninety-five postoffices throughout the country[1] and communication was in a deplorable condition, what roads there were being little more than paths and quite impassable for wheeled vehicles. Yet communication was of the utmost importance, and especially was this true in respect to the West, it being thought that commercial and political development, if not actual retention, was impossible without easier means of access. Some road construction had been accomplished by private initiative with state aid, but the problem was not really attacked, and when in 1792 Congress established a postroute between Richmond, Va., and Danville, Ky., and later one between Philadelphia, Pittsburgh, and Louisville,[2] the West became jealous of the facilities accorded the East. This feeling was encouraged by the Atlantic States being permitted by Congress to levy tonnage duties in order to effect the improvement of rivers and harbors.[3] Appropriations had also been made by Congress for lighthouses, etc., and soon the demands of the Western States were too strong to be resisted. In 1806 Congress was forced to take definite action.[4]

---

[1] American State Papers, vol. xv (Postoffice), p. 28.
[2] 1 Stat. L. 233.
[3] Lalor, Encyclopaedia of Political Science, vol. ii, p. 556.
[4] 1 Stat. L. 251.

The constitutional problem, however, had for some time engaged the attention of the leading statesmen; all admitted the necessity for federal aid, but the power of Congress was seriously questioned. In his first annual address Washington urged the encouragement of "intercourse between the distant parts of our country by a due attention to the postoffice and postroads,"[5] and repeated this recommendation in later addresses.[6] Chief Justice Jay had in 1790 given Washington his opinion, certainly entitled to great weight, that "the Congress have power to establish postroads. This would be nugatory unless it implied a power to repair these roads themselves, or compel others to do it. The former seems to be the more natural construction. Possibly the turnpike plan might gradually and usefully be introduced."[7]

But there were also many who held to a stricter construction of the Constitution. Jefferson was doubtful. Writing to Madison in 1796 he asked: "Does the power to *establish* postroads given you by Congress, mean that you shall *make* the roads, or only *select* from those already made those on which there shall be a post?" The one construction would give Congress enormous powers; the other, if inadequate, could be referred to the states for action.[8]

The question of federal power was first definitely raised in 1806 when the demands of the Western States became irresistible and Congress began the construction of the Cumberland Road, the famous highway which was to figure in the economic and political history of the United States for the next half century, and to arouse acute discussion as to the meaning of the postal clause.[9] Ohio was admitted as

[5] Richardson, vol. i, p. 66.
[6] Ibid., pp. 83, 107.
[7] Correspondence and Public Papers of John Jay (Ed. Johnston), vol. iii, p. 407.
[8] Jefferson, Writings (Ed. Ford), vol. vii, p. 63.
[9] In the discussion of this undertaking and its relation to the postoffice clause of the Constitution, I have derived much assistance from Professor J. S. Young's "A Political and Constitutional Study of the Cumberland Road" (University of Chicago Press, 1904), although this only incidentally considers the inquiry which my essay attempts.

a state in 1802 and the opportunity was seized to make a mutually advantageous arrangement by which the United States would retain the same rights as to the public domain which it possessed while Ohio was yet a territory (control of lands as yet unpaid-for and suspension of state taxes), and on the other hand, as a *quid pro quo,* a percentage of the proceeds derived from the sale of certain of the lands, should be applied to defray the cost of road construction under the auspices of the general government. Such an arrangement was first proposed by Gallatin[10] who urged "that one tenth part of the net proceeds of the lands hereafter sold by Congress shall, after deducting all expenses incident to the same, be applied towards laying out and making turnpike roads . . . under the authority of Congress, with the consent of the several states through which the same shall pass."[11]

The next action came three years later when Congress authorized the President to appoint a commission to lay out the road;[12] consent to the construction had already been given by the legislatures of Maryland and Virginia, but not by that of Pennsylvania.[13] Maryland's authorization for the improvement of postroads within the state was given in 1803 and contained a limitation to the effect that Congress was not thereby given the power "to cut down or use the timber or other material of any person or persons against his, her, or their consent,"[14]—an explicit denial of the right of eminent domain in connection with the postal power.

In January, 1807, Jefferson received the report of the commission appointed to locate the road, but the President withheld either acceptance or disapproval until he should re-

---

[10] Gallatin, Writings (Ed. Adams), vol. i, p. 76; Letter to William B. Giles, chairman of the House of Representatives Committee for admitting the North Western Territory into the Union.

[11] The proposed road fund of 10 per cent., however, was by the act which Congress passed on March 3, 1803, reduced to 5 per cent. with some restrictions as to expenditure within the state. 2 Stat. L. 226.

[12] 2 Stat. L. 357; Act of March 29, 1806.

[13] Young, The Cumberland Road, 21.

[14] Laws of Maryland, 1802–1804, ch. 115.

ceive "*full consent* to a free choice of route through the whole distance."[15] When Pennsylvania acted, its legislature detailed the powers which the United States might exercise, and stipulated that persons whose property should be taken must be given compensation; but this was sufficient for the "full consent" which Jefferson demanded before the undertaking could be begun.

Even with these limitations congressional action as to postroads had not been taken without some doubts as to its constitutionality; yet the demands for federal aid were so great and the responses so meagre that serious objection was not made. In spite of the fact that he had sanctioned appropriations for the improvement of a canal in Louisiana and a road from the Georgia frontier to New Orleans,[16] Jefferson thought that the postal clause did not grant adequate power for the construction of roads by Congress.[17] In his sixth annual message (after the passage of the Cumberland Road bill) he urged that the treasury's surplus should be applied "to the great purposes of the public education, roads, canals, and such other objects of public improvement as it may be thought proper to add to the constitutional enumeration of federal powers," but supposed that a constitutional amendment would be necessary.[18] Two years later the growing surplus led him to return to the same theme. "Shall the revenue be reduced?" he asked. "Or shall it rather be appropriated to the improvement of roads, canals, rivers, education, and other great foundations of prosperity and union, under the powers which Congress may already possess, or such amendment of the Constitution as may be approved by the states. While uncertain of the course of things the time may be advantageously employed

[15] Miscellaneous State Papers, vol. i, p. 474; Young, The Cumberland Road, p. 41.

[16] 2 Stat. L. 397, 516.

[17] On August 31, 1806, Jefferson wrote to Gallatin, commenting on the latter's plan for internal improvements, with a word of suggestion as to branches, "if it be lawful and advisable to extend our operations to them." Jefferson, Writings (Ed. Ford), vol. viii, p. 466.

[18] Richardson, vol. i, p. 409; Jefferson, vol. viii, p. 494.

in obtaining the powers necessary for a system of improvement should that be thought best."[19]

It was not, however, until during Madison's administration that the question was to become an acute one. Under Washington and Adams there had been no appropriations for roads; under Jefferson Congress had given money for the Cumberland Road, for a route from the frontier of Georgia to New Orleans and a canal in Louisiana.[20] But under Madison eleven acts were passed by Congress[21] and these caused an exhaustive and sometimes acrimonious discussion of the constitutional principles involved, with the intervention of the President through admonitory messages and one veto, on the day before he was to give up his office.

Madison's opinion as to whether the Constitution had given Congress the power to undertake the construction of roads seems not to have been absolutely consistent. Writing in *The Federalist,* he had urged as one of the advantages that the adoption of the Constitution would insure the fact that "intercourse throughout the union will be facilitated by new improvements. Roads will everywhere be shortened, and kept in better order; accommodations for travellers will be multiplied and meliorated; . . . The communication between the western and Atlantic districts, and between different parts of each, will be rendered more and more easy by those numerous canals with which the beneficence of nature has intersected our country, and which art finds it so little difficult to connect and complete."[22]

On February 5, 1796, in the House, Madison offered a resolution authorizing the President to have made a survey of the postroad from Maine to Georgia, the expense being borne by the United States.[23] Two good effects, said

[19] Richardson, vol. i, p. 456; Jefferson, vol. ix, p. 224.

[20] 2 Stat. L. 357, 397.

[21] A convenient list of these and of later laws is to be found in E. C. Nelson, "Presidential Influence on the Policy of Internal Improvements," Iowa Journal of History and Politics, vol. iv, App. A (p. 53 ff).

[22] The Federalist, No. 14.

[23] Annals of 4th Congress, 1st Sess., pp. 297, 314. A bill authorizing the survey passed the House on May 20. Ibid., p. 1415.

Madison, would accrue; "the shortest route from one place to another would be determined upon, and persons, having a certainty of the stability of the roads, would not hesitate to make improvements on them." It was to be the "commencement of an extensive work"; and during his administration Madison approved acts which appropriated over $500,000, most of it for the Cumberland Road.[24]

There had been, it is true, an intimation of a changed attitude when, in his seventh annual message (December 5, 1815), although strongly recommending the construction of roads and canals under national authority, he called it "a happy reflection that any defect of constitutional authority which may be encountered can be supplied in a mode which the Constitution itself has providently pointed out."[25] A year later he asked Congress to exercise its existing powers, and, if necessary, to resort "to the prescribed mode of enlarging them, in order to effectuate a comprehensive system of roads and canals, such as will have the effect of drawing more closely together every part of our country."[26]

Madison's decisive stand, however, was to be taken on the so-called "bonus bill," the purpose of which was to provide a permanent fund for road construction. In the famous report which Gallatin had prepared for the Senate (April 6, 1808), he had denied any right of eminent domain inhering in the United States and had declared that no road or canal could be opened without the consent of the states concerned. This fact, Gallatin argued, necessarily controlled the manner of expenditure (in the absence of constitutional amendment). He suggested two expedients: congressional undertakings with the consent of the states, or subscriptions by Congress to the shares of companies incorporated for the purpose of building highways.[27] Concerning Gallatin's second alternative, no action was taken for two years. In

---

[24] 2 Stat. L. 555, 661, 668, 670, 730, 829; 3 Stat. L. 206, 282, 315, 318, 377.

[25] Richardson, vol. i, p. 567.

[26] Richardson, vol. i, p. 576; see Farrand, vol. iii, p. 463.

[27] Miscellaneous State Papers, vol. i, p. 741.

1810, however, a Senate committee reported favorably a blanket bill which would make the government owner of one half the stock in any corporation formed to carry out the projects recommended by Gallatin in his report.[28] But the theory of the "bonus bill" was radically different.

It was reported in the House by a special committee of which Calhoun was chairman, and set aside the $1,500,000 bonus which was to be paid by the United States Bank for its charter, together with the dividend arising from the stock held by the government; there would thus be provided a permanent fund for the construction of roads and canals.

The chief argument in support of the bill was made by Calhoun.[29] He expressed no opinion as to the validity of the objection that Congress had not the power to cut a road through a state without its consent. The proposed bill did not raise that question. But, said Calhoun, "the Constitution gives to Congress the power to establish postoffices and postroads. I know that the interpretation usually given to these words confines our powers to that of designating only the postroads; but it seems to me that the word 'establish' comprehends something more," it would seem to give Congress the right to construct. Calhoun's argument is not a closely reasoned one and does not carry conviction in all respects; nevertheless, his main point upon which he lays chief weight,—that the appropriation of money by Congress is not confined to the furtherance of those powers enumerated in the Constitution,—was well taken.[30]

The bill was passed by Congress,[31] not, however, without many doubts being expressed as to its constitutionality,[32] and went to President Madison at the very close of his administration. Madison did not resort to a pocket veto and on March 3, 1817, sent a message to Congress giving the grounds for his objections to the measure. He held that

---

[28] Annals of 11th Congress, vol. ii, pp. 1401, 1443.
[29] Calhoun, Works, vol. ii, p. 193.
[30] See below, p. 75.
[31] Annals of 14th Congress, 2d Sess., p. 191.
[32] Ibid., pp. 177, 191.

the act could not be justified under the commerce or general welfare clauses, but made no use of the postal power as a possible, if not adequate source of authority. He said:

"If a general power to construct roads and canals, and to improve the navigation of water courses, with the train of powers incident thereto, be not possessed by Congress, the assent of the states in the mode provided in the bill cannot confer the power. The only cases in which the consent and cession of particular states can extend the power of Congress are those specified and provided for in the Constitution."[33]

In this message Madison did not clearly suggest a distinction between the simple power to appropriate, to appropriate and construct, with the consent of the states, and to construct against the will of local jurisdictions. Before reaching the conclusion quoted above, he had used this ambiguous language: "A restriction of the power 'to provide for the common defense and general welfare' to cases which are to be provided for by the expenditure of money would still leave within the legislative power of Congress all the great and important measures of government, money being the ordinary and necessary means of carrying them into execution."[34] Madison declared later that his veto contemplated the appropriation as well as construction; yet during his tenure he sanctioned measures providing funds for various roads.[35]

---

[33] Richardson, vol. i, p. 585; Mason, The Veto Power, p. 95. Jefferson wrote in 1817 that the President's veto was on "sound grounds; that instrument not having placed this among the enumerated objects to which they are authorized to apply the public contributions," and called the veto "a fortunate incident." Jefferson, Writings (Ed. Ford), vol. x, pp. 81, 91.

[34] Richardson, vol. i, p. 585.

[35] As late as 1830 Madison wrote: "I observe that the President, in his late veto, has seen in mine of 1817, against internal improvements by Congress, a concurrence in the power to appropriate money for the purpose. Not finding the message which he cites, I can only say that my meaning must have been unfortunately expressed or is very strangely misinterpreted. The veto on my part certainly contemplated the appropriation of money as well as the operative and jurisdictional branches of the power. And, as far as I have reference to the message, it has never been otherwise understood." Letters and Other Writings of James Madison, vol. iv, p. 86.

This distinction which Calhoun pointed out, and concerning which, in his message at least, Madison was vague, was to be stressed by Monroe and by Congress in the exhaustive debates upon the nature and extent of the power that the federal government possessed.[36] Monroe did not delay in making known his attitude and went directly to the point in his first annual message when he said:

"Disregarding early impressions, I have bestowed on the subject all the deliberation which its great importance and a just sense of my duty required, and the result is, a settled conviction, in my mind, that Congress do not possess the right. . . . In communicating this result, I cannot resist the obligation which I feel, to suggest to Congress the propriety of recommending to the states the adoption of an amendment to the Constitution, which shall give Congress the right in question."[37]

This portion of President Monroe's message was referred to a special committee in the House of Representatives which reported on December 15, 1817, in an able document.[38] The problem, said the committee, involved "a great constitutional question on the one hand," and was "intimately connected on the other, with the improvement, the prosperity, the union, and the happiness of the United States." It was argued, in brief, that Congress had the power: "1. To lay out, improve, and construct postroads through the several states, with the assent of the respective

---

[36] Before his annual message Monroe wrote to Madison: "The question respecting canals and roads is full of difficulty, growing out of what has passed on it. After all the considerations I have given it, I am fixed in the opinion, that the right is not in Congress, and that it would be improper in me, after your negative, to allow them to discuss the subject and bring in a bill for me to sign in the expectation that I would do it. I have therefore decided . . . to recommend the procuring of an amendment from the states, so as to vest the right in Congress." Writings of James Monroe, vol. vi, p. 32. Madison replied, approving this course. "*The expediency of vesting in Congress*," he said, "a power as to roads and canals, I have never doubted, and there has never been a moment when such a proposition to the states was so likely to be approved." Letters . . . of James Madison, vol. iii, p. 50.

[37] Richardson, vol. ii, p. 18.

[38] Annals of 15th Congress, 1st Sess., vol. i, p. 451.

states. 2. To open, construct, and improve military roads through the several states, with the assent of the respective states. 3. To cut canals through the several states, with their assent. . . . "

Such powers were not based, it was contended, on a liberal construction of the Constitution, nor were they dangerous in tendency and capable of working an injury to the states, for there was no recognition of a right of eminent domain or of congressional supremacy in respect to jurisdiction. Considering specifically the extent of the postal power the committee said:

"That Congress, with the assent of the states respectively, may construct and improve their postroads, under the power 'to establish postoffices and postroads' seems to be manifest both from the nature of things and from analogous constructions of the Constitution. It has been contended, indeed, that the word *establish,* in this clause of the instrument, comprehends nothing more than a mere designation of postroads. But if this be true, the important powers conferred on the general government in relation to the postoffice, might be rendered in a great measure inefficient and impracticable. . . . If the power to establish confers only the authority to designate, Congress can have no right either to keep a ferry over a deep and rapid river for the transportation of the mails, or to compel the owners of a ferry to perform that service; and yet our laws contain an act, acquiesced in for more than twenty years, imposing penalties on ferrymen for detaining the mail and on other persons for retarding or obstructing its passage. It would be difficult to discover how this power of imposing penalties can be supported, either as an original or accessory power except upon principles of more liberal construction than those now advanced. . . .

"The authority which is conferred by the Constitution to make all laws which shall be 'necessary and proper' for carrying into execution the enumerated powers, is believed to vest in the general government all the means which are essential to the complete enjoyment of the privilege of 'establishing postoffices and postroads!' Even without this clause of the Constitution the same principle would have to be applied to its construction, since according to common understanding the grant of a power implies a grant of whatever is necessary to its enjoyment. . . .

"It is indeed from the operation of these words 'necessary and proper' in the clause of the Constitution which grants accessory powers, that the 'assent of the respective states' is conceived a prerequisite to the improvement even of postroads. For, however 'necessary' such improvements might be, it might be questioned how far an interference with the state jurisdiction over its soil, against its will, might be 'proper.' Nor is this instance of an imperfect right in the general government without an analogy in the Constitution; the power of exercising jurisdiction over forts, magazines, arsenals, and dockyards, depending upon previous purchase by the United States with the consent of the states.

"Admitting then, that the Constitution confers only a right of way, and that the rights of soil and jurisdiction remain exclusively with the states respectively, yet there seems to be no sound objection to the improvement of roads with their assent."

In the long debate which followed this report upon the President's message, the opinions expressed veered between ultra-conservative and ultra-liberal positions. A middle ground was taken by Clay, whose speeches are perhaps the best on the subject.[39] He was a stanch supporter of the committee's report, contending "that the power to construct postroads is expressly granted in the power to establish postroads." "If it be," he said, "there is an end to the controversy. . . . To show that the power is expressly granted, I might safely appeal to the arguments already used to prove that the word *establish,* in this case, can mean only one thing,—the right of making." According to Clay, "to establish justice" as used in the preamble of the Constitu-

[39] Annals of 15th Cong., 1st Sess., vol. ii, p. 1366.

tion, did not compel Congress to adopt the systems then existing. "Establishment means in the preamble, as in other cases, construction, formation, creation."

When it is considered that "under the old Articles of Confederation, Congress had over the subject of postroads as much power as gentlemen allow to the existing government, that it was the general scope and spirit of the new Constitution to enlarge the powers of the general government, and that, in fact, in this very clause, the power to establish postroads is superadded to the power to establish postoffices, which was alone possessed by the former government," the argument on this point is successfully maintained.

Clay contended that "it was certainly no objection to the power that these roads might also be used for other purposes. It was rather a recommendation that other objects, beneficial to the people, might be thus obtained, though not within the words of the Constitution." For an illustration he pointed to the encouragement of manufactures under the power to levy taxes. Postroads could be devoted to "other purposes connected with the good of society."[40] Construction completed, Clay argued, Congress had a jurisdiction "concurrent with the states, over the road, for the purpose of preserving it, but for no other purpose. In regard to all matters occurring on the road, whether of crime, or contract, etc., or any object of jurisdiction unconnected with the preservation of the road, there remained to the states exclusive jurisdiction."[41]

At the conclusion of the debate several resolutions were offered and voted upon, only one receiving a majority. It recited "that Congress have power, under the Constitution, to appropriate money for the construction of postroads, military and other roads, and of canals and for the improve-

[40] Annals of 15th Cong., 1st Sess., vol. i, p. 1173. On April 27, 1816, Congress appropriated money "for the purpose of repairing and keeping in repair" certain roads under the direction of the Secretary of War. 3 Stat. L. 315. On May 20, 1826, provision was made for the repair of a postroad under the direction of the postmaster general. 4 Stat. L. 190, 154. No mention was made of the consent of the states.

[41] Annals of 15th Congress, 1st Sess., vol. i, p. 1169.

ment of water courses." In this matter Congress sanctioned the distinction between appropriation and construction. Three other resolutions were to the effect that Congress could build, generally, post and military roads; roads and canals necessary "for commerce between the states," and canals for "military purposes." These avowals of power, although they stated slightly different propositions, all intimated that the consent of the states would not be required, since each contained a proviso that private property should not be taken for public use without compensation,—a liberal attitude for this period of constitutional interpretation.[42] All of the resolutions, save the first, failed of passage by small majorities.

The consideration of Monroe's message in the Senate was very favorable to the President; there was little disposition to criticize him for having announced his views prematurely,—possibly with the intention of warning Congress,—and no attempt was made to ascertain directly the Senate's opinion on the constitutional powers of Congress. Indirectly, however, the Senate asserted its opinion through passing on a proposed amendment to the Constitution which was urged in response to Monroe's intimation that this was the proper method of dealing with the matter.

From time to time several proposed amendments to the Constitution had been introduced, and these, unlike others advocated during "the same period of conflict between the broad and strict constructionists,"[43] aimed to increase the powers of Congress, and to take away the taint of usurpation which, at least in the minds of many, was considered as attaching to the road projects either under way or seriously contemplated. Amendments empowering Congress to construct roads and canals with the consent of the states were suggested in 1813 and 1814, and on December 9, 1817, fol-

[42] Annals of 15th Cong., 1st Sess., vol. ii, p. 1380 ff.

[43] Ames, The Proposed Amendments to the Constitution of the United States during the First Century of its History, p. 20. (Report of the American Historical Association, 1896.)

lowing the advice of Monroe's message, Senator Barbour introduced in the Senate such a resolution which made state consent necessary and provided that the appropriations should be distributed "in the ratio of representation which each state shall have in the most numerous branch of the national legislature. But the portion of any state may be applied to the purpose aforesaid in any other state." When the resolution was reported, it was indefinitely postponed by a vote of 22 to 9.[44] This result showed that there was slight chance of passing any general road construction bill over the president's veto, although some of the votes against the resolution were cast on the ground that Congress already had the power.

But the advocates of road construction were not to be denied. In compliance with a resolution, Calhoun, as secretary of war, submitted to the House of Representatives on January 14, 1819, a comprehensive report on roads and canals, the necessity for them, and a scheme for construction. Calhoun, however, "thought it improper under the resolution of the House to discuss the constitutional question."[45]

The report was laid on the table[46] and although in January, 1822, the House Committee favored surveys for canals from Boston south along the Atlantic coast, and in the middle west, and a road from Washington to New Orleans, nothing became law with the exception of small appropriations for the Cumberland Road.[47] It was, however, an act for the preservation and repair of this road, passed by the House on April 29, 1822, and returned by the President on May 4, which caused him to follow his veto message with a comprehensive statement of the "Views of the President of the United States on the subject of internal improve-

[44] Annals of 15th Congress, 1st Sess., vol. i, pp. 211, 292; Ames, p. 260. Martin Van Buren while in the Senate urged a similar amendment (1824-1825) and there were others who proposed like resolutions. Ames, p. 261.

[45] See above, p. 67.

[46] Annals of 15th Congress, 2d Sess., pp. 544, 2443.

[47] 3 Stat. L. 412, 426, 500, 560, 604, 728.

ments,"[48] the most elaborate constitutional discussion ever sent to the Capitol from the White House.

Monroe was of the opinion that Congress had the right to make appropriations for roads, with the consent of the states through which they were to pass, but that it did not have sovereign and jurisdictional rights to construct roads or to repair and keep them free from obstructions. This doctrine Von Holst calls a "quibble on words," but "it has become an established one that Congress may appropriate money in aid of matters which the federal government is not constitutionally able to administer and regulate," and in this respect, therefore, Monroe was correct.[49]

The advocates of construction and of efficient jurisdiction after the roads had been made, derived the authority of Congress from several clauses in the Constitution, among them the grant "to establish postoffices and postroads." To this clause, Monroe gave an exhaustive treatment.

"What is the just import of these words, and the extent of the grant?" he asked. "The word 'establish' is the ruling term; 'postoffices and postroads' are the subjects, on which it acts. The question, therefore, is, what power is granted by that word? The sense, in which our words are commonly used, is that, in which they are to be understood in all transactions between public bodies and individuals.

---

[48] Richardson, vol. ii, p. 142. Monroe's veto was not unexpected. He had sounded a warning in his annual message of 1822 when he said that a power to execute a system of internal improvements, "confined to great national purposes and with proper limitations, would be productive of eminent advantage to our Union," and thus "thought it advisable that an amendment of the Constitution to that effect should be recommended to the several states." Ibid., vol. ii, p. 191.

[49] 1 Willoughby on the Constitution, 588. As late as 1827 Madison wrote to Monroe concerning the Cumberland Road: "I cannot assign the grounds assumed for it by Congress, or which produced his [Jefferson's] sanction. I suspect that the question of constitutionality was but slightly, if at all, examined by the former, and that the executive consent was doubtingly and hesitatingly given. Having once become a law and being a measure of singular utility, additional appropriations took place of course under the same administration, and with the accumulated impulse thus derived, were continued under the succeeding one, with less critical investigation, perhaps, than was due to the case." Madison, Works, vol. iii, p. 55.

The intention of the parties is to prevail, and there is no better way of ascertaining it, than by giving to the terms used their ordinary import."

Among enlightened citizens, Monroe went on, there would be no difference of opinion; "all of them would answer, that a power was thereby given to Congress to fix on the towns, court-houses, and other places, throughout our Union, at which there should be postoffices; the routes by which the mails should be carried from one postoffice to another, so as to diffuse intelligence as extensively, and to make the institution as useful, as possible; to fix the postage to be paid on every letter and packet thus carried to support the establishment; and to protect the postoffices and mails from robbery, by punishing those, who should commit the offence. The idea of a right to lay off the roads of the United States, on a general scale of improvement; to take the soil from the proprietor by force; to establish turnpikes and tolls, and to punish offenders in the manner stated above, would never occur to any such person. The use of the existing road, by the stage, mail carrier, or postboy, in passing over it, as others do, is all that would be thought of; the jurisdiction and soil remaining to the state, with a right in the state, or those authorized by its legislature, to change the road at pleasure."

This interpretation, the message went on to declare, was supported by the modification of the postal grant in the Articles of Confederation, as it appeared in the Constitution. "Had it been intended to convey a more enlarged power in the Constitution," said Monroe, "than had been granted in the Confederation, surely the same controlling term [establish] would not have been used; or other words would have been added, to show such intention, and to mark the extent, to which the power should be carried. . . . It would be absurd to say, that, by omitting from the Constitution any portion of the phraseology, which was deemed important in the Confederation, the import of that term was enlarged, and with it the powers of the Constitution, in a proportional degree, beyond what they were in the Confederation. The right to exact postage and to protect the postoffices and mails from robbery, by punishing the offenders, may fairly be considered, as incidents to the grant, since, without it, the object of the grant might be defeated. Whatever is absolutely necessary to the accomplishment of the object of the grant, though not specified, may fairly be considered as included in it. Beyond this the doctrine of incidental power cannot be carried." Monroe then enters upon a consideration of what the colonists and framers of the Constitution understood to be comprehended in the postal power, and concludes:

"If the United States possessed the power contended for under this grant, might they not, in adopting the roads of the individual states for the carriage of the mail, as has been done, assume jurisdiction over them, and preclude a right to interfere with or alter them? Might they not establish turnpikes, and exercise all the other acts of sovereignty, above stated, over such roads, necessary to protect them from injury, and defray the expense of repairing them? Surely, if the right exists, these consequences necessarily followed, as soon as the road was established. The absurdity of such a pretension must be apparent to all, who examine it. In this way, a large portion of the territory of every state might be taken from it; for there is scarcely a road in any state, which will not be used for the transportation of the mail. A new field for legislation and internal government would thus be opened."[50]

[50] The validity of Monroe's argument is treated below, p. 81. Perhaps it may not be amiss to add that I have not attempted an exhaustive consideration of congressional activity in respect to road construction. This has been done by Nelson, Presidential Influence on the Policy of Internal Improvements, and Young, A Political and Constitutional Study of the Cumberland Road. There are also excellent and less specialized accounts in Babcock, The Rise of American Nationality, ch. xv, Turner, The Rise of the New West, ch. xiii (American Nation, vols. 13 and 14), and Schouler, History of the United States, vol. iii. My sole purpose has been to treat congressional action and presidential opinion from their constitutional aspects in relation to the power to establish postoffices and postroads.

While the President's attitude stopped Congress from actually constructing roads, frequent appropriations were granted to be applied under the direction of the states. Perhaps the most important of these was in the act passed in 1824 to have surveys made of such roads and canals as in the opinion of the President were of value for military, commercial and postal purposes.[51]

Conflict over the constitutional problem, and the distinction between appropriation and construction, were, however, abandoned by John Quincy Adams who was a stanch advocate of federal aid,[52] but the discussion was revived by Jackson, who vetoed six bills,[53] the most important of which provided for a government subscription of $150,000 to purchase stock in the Maysville, Washington, Paris and Lexington Turnpike Company, a Kentucky corporation. The action of the President did not come as a surprise for in his first annual message he had told Congress that the mode of internal improvements, "hitherto adopted, has by many of our fellow citizens been deprecated as an infraction of the constitution, while by others it has been viewed as inexpedient. All feel that it has been employed at the expense of harmony in the legislative councils."[54]

Furthermore, Jackson thoroughly disapproved of the government's becoming a minority stockholder in a semi-private enterprise which would receive profits through the payment of tolls. He held it to be not only "highly expedient, but indispensably necessary, that a previous amendment of the Constitution, delegating the necessary power and defining and restricting its exercise with reference to the sovereignty of the states, should be made."[55] Otherwise there would be a continuance of congressional uncertainty as to the existence of the power. He considered the general question in

[51] 4 Stat. L. 71; for the list of appropriations, see Nelson, p. 57; see also Lalor, Cyclopaedia of Political Science (Internal Improvements), vol. ii, p. 568.

[52] Richardson, vol. ii, p. 281.

[53] Mason, The Veto Power, pp. 143, 145.

[54] Richardson, vol. ii, p. 452.

[55] Ibid., vol. ii, p. 492.

two aspects: (1) as "to the power of making internal improvements within the limits of a state, with the right of territorial jurisdiction, sufficient at least for their preservation and use" and (2) as to the power of "appropriating money in aid of such works when carried on by a state or by a company in virtue of state authority, surrendering the claim of jurisdiction."[56] He believed Congress could appropriate directly for *national,* not *local,* purposes; the other power he firmly denied.

After Jackson there were other vetoes of internal improvement bills, but they were based largely upon the distinction between national and local objects. Road construction, moreover, gave way to river and harbor development, and there was little, if any, discussion of the meaning of the postal clause. Congress asserted a broad power over postroads designated by it, and there was little objection; on the few occasions that the matter came before the courts, the power was sustained. In 1862 Congress gave the President authority when in his judgment the public safety required its exercise, to take possession of all railroads and telegraphs and to place their employees under military control, so that the lines would be "considered as a postroad and a part of the military establishment of the United States, subject to all the rules and restrictions imposed by the rules and articles of war."[57] Any interference with the exercise of this authority was made a crime. Compensation to the railroad and telegraph companies was to be fixed by three commissioners, subject to approval by Congress. This authorization, however, was based upon the war, as well as on the postal power, and when Congress came to charter railroads and bridge companies, it based its right largely on the commerce clause, with the postal and war grants as ancillary sources.[58]

Recent evidences of congressional action, based upon the

---

[56] Richardson, vol. iii, p. 119; Bassett, Life of Andrew Jackson, vol. ii, pp. 483-495.
[57] 12 Stat. L. 334.
[58] See also Act of July 1, 1862; 12 Stat. L. 489.

postroads clause, are to be seen in the good roads movement, and in 1912 Congress appropriated five hundred thousand dollars for "improving the condition of roads to be selected by them [the secretary of agriculture and the postmaster general] over which rural delivery is or may hereafter be established, such improvement to be for the purpose of ascertaining the increase in the territory which could be served by each carrier as a result of such improvement, the possible increase of the number of delivery days in each year," etc. But it is provided that the state in which the improvements are to be made "shall furnish double the amount of money for the improvement of the road or roads so selected."[59] The results of the scheme have not been very satisfactory,[60] but proposals are made for other, and more extensive federal undertakings. Finally it is possible, in some measure at least, to base upon the postal power the Act of March 12, 1914, which authorizes "the president of the United States to locate, construct and operate railroads in the Territory of Alaska."[61]

Judicial Determinations.—The power of Congress to construct roads and canals did not, in the early days of its assertion and denial, come before the Supreme Court of the United States; in fact, the question has never been directly passed upon by the Court, and long before it was incidentally considered, largely in the cases upholding the right of eminent domain and its delegation to railroad corporations with federal charters, the constitutional problem, as Madison said in rejecting the bank bill of 1814, was "precluded by repeated recognitions, under varied circumstances, of the validity of the exercise of a power to establish a bank by Congress, in acts of the legislative, executive, and judicial branches of the government, accompanied by indications in

---

[59] 37 Stat. L. 552.

[60] Sloane, Party Government in the United States of America, p. 316.

[61] Public, No. 69, 63d Congress; Act of March 12, 1914. See also 63d Cong., 1 Sess., S. Rept. No. 65; 63d Cong., 2d Sess., H. Rept. No. 341, and Weems, "Government Railroads in Alaska," North American Review, April, 1914.

different modes of a concurrence of the general will of the nation."[62] Such a test, however, is by no means adequate.

For a time the question of congressional power was acute, and its existence was not acknowledged, even by some who cannot be called strict constructionists. The opinions held by Congress and the executive have already been reviewed; but Monroe's elaborate veto message on the "gate bill" gave the Supreme Court justices an opportunity to express their views informally, for he sent a copy of his paper to each member of the Court. In his reply Justice Johnson intimated that the doctrine of McCulloch v. Maryland[63] committed the Court to upholding a power in Congress to construct roads for military and postal purposes; Marshall considered the question one "on which many divide in opinion, but all will admit that your views are profound and that you have thought much on the subject." Story was noncommittal, and thus one of the few attempts to get an informal expression of opinion from the Supreme Court was a failure.[64]

It is difficult to see how, logically, there can be any doubt as to a very wide authority in Congress. A fair interpretation of the word "establish" comprehends "construction" or at least something more than "designation"; otherwise it would have been futile for the Articles of Confederation and the Constitution to give Congress powers under which it has undertaken to "establish" navy hospitals, trading houses with the Indians, inferior courts, rules of capture, and regulations of trade. The second portion of the postal clause did not appear in the Articles of Confederation, and the grant in the Constitution was absolute, with no limita-

[62] Richardson, vol. ii, p. 555.

[63] 4 Wheat. 316 (1819).

[64] In his Commentaries, Story devotes twenty pages to an exposition of both sides of the controversy and concludes: "The reader must decide for himself, upon the preponderance of the argument." Vol. iii, p. 46. The incident of submitting the message to the Supreme Court is given in detail by Schouler, History of the United States, vol. iii, p. 254 ff. As to advisory opinions, see 1 Willoughby on the Constitution, 13, and Thayer, Cases on Constitutional Law, vol. i, p. 175.

tions as to state action. A restricted interpretation, applied to the first part of the clause, as demanded by consistency, would give Congress authority to provide postoffices, but without mails, carriers, routes, secure transmission, or revenue. That Congress in fact had the power to construct roads has been made evident, I think, by the debates on the various measures that were proposed.

But as has been seen in the legislation concerning the Cumberland Road, the consent of the states was required before construction could be started, and limitations were imposed on the federal power. So also, it was at first maintained that Congress did not have the right to keep the roads open, in repair, and to impose tolls for their use, whether they had been constructed under national authority or had simply been designated as mail routes. For example, the Act of March 26, 1804, provided "that whenever it shall be made to appear to the satisfaction of the postmaster general that any road established by this or any former act, as a postroad, is obstructed by fences, gates or bars, other than those lawfully used on turnpike roads, to collect their toll, and not kept in good repair with proper bridges and ferries, where the same may be necessary it shall be the duty of the postmaster general to report the same to Congress, with such information as can be obtained, to enable Congress to establish some other road, instead of it, in the same main direction."[65]

In 1812 Gallatin made a report to the President on the Cumberland Road and referred to the necessity of levying

[65] 2 Stat. L. 275, 277. In 1810 the postmaster general was given authority to "provide for the carriage of the mail on all postroads that are or may be established by law," and to "direct the route or road, when there are more than one between places designated by law for a postroad, which route shall be considered as the postroad"; and the lines designated in contracts for carrying the mail were to be considered postroads within the provisions of the act. 2 Stat. L. 592. But in 1825 while the authority of the postmaster general to designate different routes was continued, there was a further provision that in cases not covered by contracts, "the road, on which such mail shall be transported, shall become a postroad and so continue until the transportation thereon shall cease." 4 Stat. L. 102.

tolls sufficient to keep certain portions in repair; but this, he said, could be done "only under the authority of the state of Maryland."[66] The next year the superintendent of the road reported to Gallatin that he expected the Maryland legislature to pass a law, "authorizing the President to receive toll, for the purpose of repairing the road, and likewise against abuses which are common on all roads of the kind to prevent which laws have been found necessary."[67] Secretary Dallas was of the same opinion, and in 1815 told the House Committee on the Cumberland Road that Congress had no authority to make provision for tolls and the prevention of abuses. "They can only proceed," he said, "from the legislatures of the states through which the road passes, and consist of an authority for the erection of toll gates, and the collection of a toll sufficient to defray the expenses of repair, and the infliction of penalties upon persons who shall cut, break up, or otherwise destroy or injure the road."[68]

The House Committee, however, held that since a compact had been entered into between the federal government and the states, Congress had the right to legislate in order to carry out its undertaking to open and maintain the road. "If the right to punish these offences belongs to the national government," said the committee, "it may be effected without the passage of any law, by an indictment or information in the courts of the United States, or by enacting statutory provisions fixing the penalties, it being a fundamental right of the judiciary inherent in every government to punish all offences against the laws passed in pursuance of a delegated power independently of express legislative sanctions."[69]

After President Monroe's veto, the Cumberland Road became sadly in need of repairs, and again Congress considered the question of jurisdiction,—whether the right to *preserve*

[66] Miscellaneous State Papers, vol. ii, p. 175.
[67] Ibid., p. 205.
[68] Ibid., p. 272.
[69] Ibid., p. 301. See U. S. v. Hudson & Goodwin, 7 Cranch 32 (1812).

was incidental to the right to *establish*. The states passed laws to protect the road against injuries and appropriated money for improvements, but the sums provided were inadequate[70] and soon a disposition was shown to consent to the assumption by Congress of complete control over the Road. The Pennsylvania legislature passed a resolution (1828) giving the federal government permission to collect tolls within the commonwealth, with the reservation that the whole amount collected should be devoted to repairs.[71]

Monroe had desired cooperation between the national and local authorities. In his message of December 2, 1823, he urged "an arrangement with the several states through which the Road passes, to establish tolls, each within its limits, for the purpose of defraying the expense of future repairs and providing also by suitable penalties for its protection against future injuries."[72] This portion of the message was considered by the House Committee on Roads and Canals, whose opinion it was that Congress had itself the right to charge tolls and punish offences; the committee could not approve of an arrangement by which the states might charge tolls: uniformity and one jurisdiction were eminently desirable.[73] Yet in 1828–1829 when the whole question of control was again threshed out in Congress, any federal right, either absolutely or by virtue of state permission, to charge tolls, was still denied. Congress simply appropriated $100,000 for the repair of the road; Monroe's distinction between *appropriation* and *control* was adhered to.[74]

The states, moreover, still asserted plenary authority. In 1833 the Maryland legislature gave the President authority to make a change in the Cumberland Road[75] and in 1834 Illinois consented to the extension of the national road "through the territory of said state so as to cross the

[70] Young, The Cumberland Road, p. 79.
[71] Laws of Pennsylvania, 1827–28, p. 500.
[72] Richardson, vol. ii, p. 217.
[73] 18th Cong., 1st Sess., House Rept. No. 118.
[74] Act of March 3, 1829; 4 Stat. L. 363.
[75] Laws of Maryland, 1831–1832, ch. 55.

Mississippi River at the town of Alton and no other point."[76] For various reasons the road was not constructed, but Congress was several times memorialized to take the desired action[77] and in 1844 the Senate Committee on Roads and Canals, having under consideration a bill to extend the highway to Alton, made a favorable recommendation and pointed out the fact that the consent of the states affected was a necessary preliminary before actual construction could begin.

"The right of the state of Illinois to give or withhold her assent to the construction of the road within her limits," said the committee's report, "cannot be questioned in view of the course pursued by the general government to obtain the consent of other states."[78] Reports to identical effect were made during the second session of the 28th Congress (January 15, 1845) and the second session of the 29th Congress (January 16, 1847),[79] the second report being accompanied by a strong letter from Senator Semple of Illinois, who pointed out that his state would never consent to any route other than the one which had been recommended in 1834.

Meanwhile definitive action had been taken during Jackson's administration, as a result of his determined opposition to internal improvements and denial of federal authority to construct roads. "Annual appropriations for the repair of the road were being made, but this method could not continue indefinitely, inasmuch as tolls could not be levied by the United States for repairs. Because of the lack of jurisdiction, a resort to state control, with the consent of Congress became an absolute necessity."[80] Acts of the Pennsylvania, Maryland, Ohio and Virginia legislatures were, therefore, passed, and congressional assent was given to the erection of toll gates and repairs by the states, with the

---

[76] 13 Congressional Debates, 1132.

[77] 24th Cong., 1st Sess., Sen. Doc. No. 196.

[78] 28th Cong., 1st Sess., Sen. Doc. No. 324, p. 7.

[79] 28th Cong., 2d Sess., Sen. Doc. No. 41, and 29th Cong., 2d Sess., Sen. Doc. No. 70.

[80] Young, The Cumberland Road, p. 87.

provision in the compact that no charge should be made for the passage of United States mails, troops or property. In 1879 the control of the states was made complete and unreserved. Yet the original acts of surrender recognized "either a proprietary or jurisdictional interest, or both, in the United States, as follows: (1) something was surrendered; (2) surrender was made by 'compacts' which regulated the number of toll gates and the rates of toll; (3) provision was made for the United States to resume its proprietary or jurisdictional interest at pleasure."[81]

But before the legal questions arising out of this surrender were passed upon by the Supreme Court of the United States, the whole problem of congressional power and the rights of the states was carefully considered by the Kentucky Court of Appeals, whose opinion,[82] treating points *primae impressionis,* is remarkably well considered. The particular question to be decided was whether a contractor for carrying the mail between points within the state on a turnpike road had any right of exemption from the tolls, exacted under the company's charter from other persons for the transit of their horses and stages. The court held that the tolls should be paid.

It recognized that the postal power "being necessarily exclusive, plenary and supreme, no state can constitutionally do, or authorize to be done, any act which may frustrate, counteract, or impair the proper and effectual exercise of it by national authority. From these axiomatic truths it follows as a plain corollary that the general government has the right to transport the national mail *whenever* and *wherever* the national Congress, in the *constitutional* exercise of its delegated power over *postoffices* and *postroads* shall have prescribed." But, said the court, this power was not unlimited, and could not appropriate private property for public

---

[81] Young, p. 98, and *passim* for an able account of the whole controversy over jurisdiction. I have here attempted to present only the points necessary for an understanding of the constitutional problems that the courts were called upon to consider.

[82] Dickey v. Maysville, etc., Co., 7 Dana (37 Ky.) 113 (1838).

use without just compensation. If the turnpike was considered as private property in view of the company's franchise, tolls should be paid by the mail contractor; considering the turnpike as a public state road, the court reached the same conclusion, which, it pointed out, would not have been modified had Congress seen fit to designate this particular road as a mail route. Anyone doubting the logic of this, the court said, "should also doubt whether his own house might not be taken and used as a postoffice without his consent and without any compensation."

The court then proceeded, *obiter,* to explain its understanding of the postroads power. According to reason and philology, the import of "establish" was declared to be, not merely "designate" but "found, prepare, make, institute and confirm." "So too," the court held, "as roads and good roads are indispensable to the effectual establishment of postroads, the supreme power to 'establish postroads' necessarily includes the power to make, repair and preserve such roads as may be suitable. . . ." Congress therefore was considered to have the power to open roads and build bridges when necessary; there was no question of constitutional right, simply of expediency.[83]

"Unless Congress shall elect to exercise its right of eminent domain, and buy a state road, or make one, or help to make or repair it, the constitution gives no authority to use it as a postroad without the consent of the state or the owner, without making just compensation for the use." Here was acknowledgment of an authority more far reaching than even the more liberal contemporary opinion gave to Congress; the court recognized a right of eminent domain to take over a road, but until this was exercised, the mails were subject to tolls.

When, seven years later, the Supreme Court of the United States passed upon the toll question which arose under the

---

83 "Every postroad is a national road," said the court. "So far as it is a postroad, it is as national as the Chesapeake Bay or the Mississippi River."

compact ceding the Cumberland Road to the states,[84] there was the same opportunity to make a definite pronouncement as to the authority of Congress to engage in road construction; in its opinion, however, the Court made no use of this opportunity, although a dissentient justice voiced his views that the power of Congress was not so great as that asserted in the Dickey case.

The act of the Ohio legislature in taking over the Cumberland Road specifically provided that tolls should not be collected for the passage of the mails; but the Pennsylvania law was more general, declaring that "no toll shall be received or collected for the passage of any wagon or carriage laden with the property of the United States. . . ." The Maryland act was precisely the same as this, while the Virginia statute followed the Ohio law. In 1836, however, Pennsylvania declared that the exemption should be only in proportion to the amount of property belonging to the United States, and "that in all cases of wagons, carriages, stages or other modes of conveyance, carrying the United States mail, with passengers or goods, such wagon, stage, or other mode of conveyance shall pay half-toll upon such modes of conveyance."

The validity of this legislation was the question presented to the Supreme Court, and in its decision the Court could well have entered upon a discussion of the power of Congress in the premises. But Chief Justice Taney, who delivered the opinion, was at pains to point out, "that the constitutional power of the general government to construct this road is not involved in the case before us; nor is the court called upon to express any opinion on that subject; nor to inquire what were the rights of the United States in the road previous to the compacts hereinbefore mentioned."

Taney simply held, therefore, that "the United States have unquestionably a property in the mails"; that this property was exempted from the payment of tolls by the terms of the compact, but this exemption should not apply to

[84] Seabright v. Stokes, 3 Howard 151 (1845).

other property in the same vehicle, nor to any person unless in the service of the United States. Finally, in answer to the objection that small parcels might be sent by a number of conveyances to relieve them from the payment of tolls, Taney held that "the United States cannot claim an exemption for more carriages than are necessary for the safe, speedy, and convenient conveyance of the mail."

From Taney's judgment, Justice McLean dissented, primarily on the ground that "the mail of the United States is not the property of the United States," and that charging tolls for its passage was not in violation of the compact. Justice Daniels, however, objected upon different grounds, and declared that it was necessary to consider "the operation and effect of the compact insisted upon as controlled and limited by the powers of both contracting parties."

"I hold then," he declared, "that neither Congress nor the federal government in the exercise of all or any of its powers or attributes possesses the power to construct roads, nor any other description of what have been called internal improvements within the limits of the states. That the territory and soil of the several states appertain to them by title paramount to the Constitution, and cannot be taken, save with the exception of those portions which might be ceded for the seat of the federal government and for sites permitted to be purchased for forts, arsenals, dockyards, etc. That the power of the federal government to acquire, and that of the states to cede, to that government portions of their territory, are by the Constitution limited to the instances above adverted to, and that these powers can neither be enlarged, nor modified, but in virtue of some new faculty to be imparted by amendments of the Constitution.

"I believe that the authority vested in Congress by the Constitution to establish postroads, confers no right to open new roads, but implies nothing beyond a discretion in the government in the regulations it may make for the post-office department for the selection amongst the various routes, whilst they continue in existence, of those along which it may be deemed most judicious to have the mails transported. I do not believe that this power given to Congress expresses or implies anything peculiar in relation to the means or modes of transporting the public mail, or refers to any supposed means or modes of transportation beyond the usual manner existing and practised in the country, and certainly it cannot be understood to destroy or in anywise to affect the proprietary rights belonging to individuals or companies vested in those roads. It guarantees to the government the right to avail itself of the facilities offered by those roads for the purposes of transportation, but imparts to it no exclusive rights—it puts the government upon the footing of others who would avail themselves of the same facilities."

For these reasons, "the government could legally claim no power to collect tolls, no exemption from tolls, nor any diminution of tolls in their favor, purely in consequence of their having expended money on the road, and without the recognition by Pennsylvania of that expenditure as a condition in any contract they might make with that state." Nevertheless the United States could contract with Pennsylvania, and so Justice Daniels examined the terms of the agreement, coming to the conclusion that by its terms, United States mail was not exempt from toll charges.[85]

While the authority of the majority opinion in this case is somewhat lessened by the fact that the argument was as to the meaning of the compact, it was held, impliedly at least, that in order to carry out one of its delegated powers, —the establishment of postoffices and postroads,—the United

[85] See also Neil v. Ohio, 3 How. 720 (1845), and Achison v. Huddleson, 12 How. 293 (1851). Congress, under an act approved February 25, 1867, granted the state of Oregon certain lands for the construction of a military road, with the reservation that it should be free for the passage of federal property, troops or mails. An incorporated company undertook construction of the road, but was not permitted to charge tolls. It was provided in the grant that bridges should be constructed to permit the use of the road by wagons. This was done by parties other than the road company, and when mail contractors paid them tolls they had a right of action for reimbursement from the feasor company. Schutz v. Dalles Military Road Co., 7 Or. 259 (1879).

States might, by compact, enter upon a scheme of internal improvements. Furthermore, the court, by holding that the general government had the right to enter into the compact of surrender, recognized an original federal interest in the Cumberland Road. The clear import of the majority opinion is, I think, that if Taney had considered it necessary to pass upon the point, Congress would have been accorded the right to construct postroads, and this would have included authority to charge tolls for the use of the highways by others than the postoffice department.[86]

These adjudications were carried a long step further when the Supreme Court asserted the federal right of eminent domain which had been foreshadowed in the Dickey case, but not exercised by Congress.[87] In 1864 the Northern Pacific Railroad was incorporated, and lands were granted to aid in the construction, but the act provided that the company "shall obtain the consent of the legislature of any state through which any portion of said railroad line may pass, previous to commencing the construction thereof." Congress reserved the right to appeal or amend the act, "to secure to the government at all times (but particularly in time of war) the use and benefits of the same for postal, military and other purposes."[88] In 1868, however, Congress undertook improvements in the Mississippi River, and authorized its agents to take possession of the necessary materials "after having first paid or secured to be paid, the

---

[86] Young, The Cumberland Road, p. 100. The question of state tolls on mail carriers will be treated in the chapter on "The Power of the States to Interfere with the Mails."

[87] "The government of the United States cannot construct a postroad within a state of this union without its consent; but Congress may declare, that is, establish, such a road already opened and made a public highway by the direct or indirect authority of the state. . . . The United States have the mere right of transit over these roads for the purpose of carrying the mail, and in case of obstructing this right their laws provide an adequate remedy. . . . The act of Congress making all railroads postroads means only such as have charters from the several states." Cleveland, P. & A. R. Co. v. Franklin Canal Co., 5 Fed. Cas. 1044 (1853).

[88] 13 Stat. L. 365.

value thereof which may have been ascertained in the mode provided by the laws of the state."[89]

When the question came before the courts there was little hesitancy in holding that Congress had a right of eminent domain. The Circuit Court for the Southern District of Ohio declared that "the constitutional provisions giving to Congress authority to establish postoffices and postroads, and to make all laws for carrying into effect the enumerated powers, taken together with the declaration that all laws made in pursuance of the Constitution shall be the supreme law of the land, invest Congress with authority to condemn lands situated within a state for use as a postoffice site."[90] A holding to the same effect was made by the Supreme Court of the United States which declared:

"It is true, this power of the federal government has not heretofore been exercised adversely; but the non-user of a power does not disprove its existence. . . . If the United States have the power, it must be complete in itself. It can neither be enlarged nor diminished by a state. Nor can any state prescribe the manner in which it must be exercised. The consent of a state can never be a condition precedent to its enjoyment."[91]

But before this right of eminent domain was recognized, a broad legislative control had been assumed over the highways of the country. In 1838 Congress declared "that each and every railroad within the limits of the United States which now is, or hereafter may be made and completed, shall be a postroute,"[92] and in 1856, the Supreme Court (under the commerce clause, however) sanctioned a further extension.

Bridges across the Ohio River at Wheeling were alleged by the State of Pennsylvania to be an obstruction of navigation and their removal was ordered by the Supreme Court.

---

[89] 15 Stat. L. 124.

[90] U. S. v. Inlots, 26 Fed. Cas. 482 (1873). See also Trombley v. Humphrey, 23 Mich. 472 (1871), and 1 Kent's Comm. 268, Note A.

[91] Kohl v. U. S., 91 U. S. 367 (1875).

[92] 5 Stat. L. 283.

The decree had not been executed when, by act of Congress (1852), the bridges were "declared to be lawful structures in their present positions and elevations, and shall be so held and taken to be, anything in the law or laws of the United States to the contrary notwithstanding," and further, "that the said bridges be declared to be and are established post-roads for the passage of the mails of the United States."

Later, the main bridge being blown down, the Supreme Court granted an injunction restraining the reconstruction. The company disregarded the order and upon motions by the plaintiff to attach the defendant's property for contempt, and by the company to dissolve the injunction, the Supreme Court held that the act of Congress vacated the decree and superseded its effect and operation. The Court said:

"We do not enter upon the question, whether or not Congress possess the power, under the authority of the Constitution, 'to establish postoffices and postroads' to legalize this bridge; for, concluding that no such powers can be derived from this clause, it must be admitted that it is, at least, necessarily included in the powers conferred to regulate commerce among the several states."[93]

By the act of March 2, 1861,[94] moreover, the monopoly provisions of earlier statutes were extended to all post-routes, already or thereafter established, but letter carrier routes within cities did not become postroads until so declared by Congress in 1872, and at the present time, in addition to railroads and routes for the collection and delivery of

---

93 Pennsylvania v. Wheeling Bridge Co., 18 How. 421 (1856); see also 13 How. 518 (1852).

94 12 Stat. L. 205. See Blackham v. Gresham, 16 Fed. Rep. 609 (1883), and U. S. v. Kochersperger, 26 Fed. Cas. 803 (1860), where it was said: "The public streets of a municipal town over which the mail may be carried in any of the routes established by Congress as postroads, are doubtless, postroads for the passage of the mail. Whether the streets of such a town can be established by Congress as postroads for any other purpose is questionable. . . . So far as the prohibition of private letter carrying within the limits of such a town may be concerned, the legislative power which is wanting under the head of postroads, may, perhaps, be incidental to the execution of the power to establish postoffices. If this be so, the point may be of little ultimate practical importance." Blackham v. Gresham upheld the act of 1861.

the mail, the following are established as postroads: all waters of the United States, canals, and plank roads during the time the mail is carried thereon; "the road on which the mail is carried to supply any courthouse which may be without a mail, and the road on which the mail is carried under contract made by the postmaster general for extending the line of posts to supply mails to postoffices not on any established route, during the time such mail is carried thereon"; and "all public roads and highways while kept up and maintained as such."[95] In order to insure the safe passage of the mails, the federal government may take all necessary measures to remove obstructions and prevent depredations, even on the public streets of a town.

Finally, under three grants in the Constitution,—to regulate commerce, to establish postoffices and postroads, and to raise and support armies,—Congress has chartered transcontinental railway companies and bridge companies. It has, moreover, granted to these corporations the power of eminent domain to be exercised without the consent or permission of the states. In holding that the franchises of the Union Pacific Railroad Company were federal franchises, properly granted, and beyond the power of the state to tax, the Supreme Court said:

"It cannot at the present day be doubted that Congress under the power to regulate commerce among the several states, as well as to provide for postal accommodations and military exigencies, had authority to pass these laws. The power to construct, or to authorize individuals or corporations to construct, national highways and bridges from state to state, is essential to the complete control and regulation of interstate commerce. Without authority in Congress to establish and maintain such highways and bridges, it would be without authority to regulate one of the most important adjuncts of commerce. This power in former times was exerted to a very limited extent, the Cumberland or National Road being the most notable instance. Its exertion was but

[95] See Postal Laws and Regulations of 1913, p. 605.

little called for, as commerce was then mostly conducted by water, and many of our statesmen entertained doubts as to the existence of the power to establish ways of communication by land. But since, in consequence of the expansion of the country, the multiplication of its products, the invention of railroads and locomotion by steam, land transportation has so vastly increased, a sounder consideration of the subject has prevailed, and led to the conclusion that Congress has plenary power over the whole subject. Of course, the authority of Congress over the territories of the United States, and its power to grant franchises exercisable therein, are, and ever have been, undoubted. But the wider power was very freely exercised, and much to the general satisfaction, in the creation of the vast system of railroads connecting the East with the Pacific, traversing states as well as territories and employing the agency of state as well as federal corporations."[96]

Early attempts, then, by Congress to furnish postal facilities and open up communication through the construction of highways for the carriage of the mails, met with denials that the power "to establish postroads" meant more than the power to designate the roads to be used, and that, even if this were not so, any action could be taken without the consent of the states whose territory was to be used. To permit national undertakings, however, Monroe developed the distinction that Congress might appropriate for roads to be laid out with the consent of the states, but that the national government had no jurisdictional rights to construct, repair or keep the highways free from obstructions. This distinction, which Von Holst called a "quibble on words," was abandoned by John Quincy Adams, who was a stanch advocate of federal aid, but was revived by Jackson, who believed that appropriations could be made for *national,* but not for *local* purposes. In Congress, during the whole of this period, various views were expressed, but the better

[96] California v. Pacific Railroad Co., 127 U. S. 1 (1888). Cases involving these points will be treated in a later chapter on "The Extension of Federal Control over Postroads."

opinion, accepted by the authority, if not by the majority, of the speakers, was that Congress had powers (occasionally exercised) which were broader than the executives were disposed to concede.

The continued assertion by the states of plenary authority and the failure of Congress to adopt any successful plan by which the Cumberland Road might be kept in repair, led to compacts of surrender under which the national authorities gave up all control over this highway. The meaning of these compacts was examined by the Supreme Court of the United States, and the plain implication of the decisions (although definite expressions were not necessary for the determination of the particular questions presented) is that Congress had the right to construct postroads and to charge tolls for their use by others than postal officials. This power had already been conceded in an illuminating opinion by the Kentucky Court of Appeals, and the subsequent decisions recognizing a right of eminent domain in the federal government and sanctioning the federal incorporation of railway and bridge companies, are conclusive authority that Congress had the power which the more liberal of its members asserted, but which the states and occasional executives denied. That the power to *establish* postroads comprehends the power to *construct* (compensation being made to the states), to levy tolls, and to repair and keep free from obstructions, has thus been assured by judicial decisions as well as by a fair interpretation of the words of the grant; and any fancied taint of unconstitutionality has been removed from laws which Congress passed under its plenary power "to establish postroads," but which exceeded the limitations laid down by the strict constructionists, and did not come before the Supreme Court for a determination of their validity.

CHAPTER IV

LIMITATIONS ON THE POSTAL POWER

Like all grants to Congress, the postal power is not unrestrained, but, as the Supreme Court has expressed it, the difficulty in setting limits beyond which it may not go, arises, "not from want of power in Congress to prescribe the regulations as to what shall constitute mail matter, but from the necessity of enforcing them consistently with the rights reserved to the people, of far greater importance than the transportation of the mail."[1] One, and perhaps the most important, of these rights is involved when restrictions are applied to periodical publications (particularly in reference to obscene matter and lottery tickets), and the question is at once raised as to the freedom of the press, guaranteed against abridgment by the second clause of the first amendment to the Federal Constitution.[2] The extent to which this limitation has been ignored is a moot question. On the one hand, we have the confident assertion of Von Holst[3] that "the freedom of the press has become a part of the flesh and blood of the American people to such an extent, and is so conditioned by the democratic character of their political and social life, that a successful attack upon it, no matter what legal authority it might have on its side, is impossible. Even the gigantic power of slavocracy gave up the battle as hopeless after the first onslaught."

On the other hand, Hannis Taylor in his recent work on the American Constitution remarks that "little need be said

[1] Ex parte Jackson, 96 U. S. 727 (1878).

[2] "Congress shall make no law . . . abridging the freedom of speech or of the press." An executive order, deriving its validity from an act of Congress would, of course, be illegal if abridging the liberty of the press, even though the act itself did not.

[3] Von Holst, Constitutional History of the United States, vol. ii, p. 127.

as to the clause forbidding Congress to pass any law 'abridging the freedom of the press,' as that clause has been removed from the Constitution, so far as the mails are concerned, by the judgment rendered in 1892, *In Re Rapier*."[4] And this extreme view may be said to have received some support from a recent decision of the Supreme Court which upheld the power of Congress to compel newspapers to publish certain information concerning their internal affairs, under penalty, for refusal, of being denied the advantages of low second class rates.[5] Which, then, is the correct view as to the inviolability or abrogation of this constitutional guarantee in relation to the mails?

Freedom of the Press.—In the Convention which framed the Federal Constitution, Mr. Pinckney, on August 20, 1787, submitted a number of propositions among which was a guarantee that "the liberty of the Press shall be inviolably preserved."[6] The propositions were referred to the Committee of Detail, and when the question again came up for consideration on September 14, Mr. Pinckney and Mr. Gerry "moved to insert a declaration that the liberty of the Press should be inviolably observed." This motion was lost, Mr. Sherman remarking that "it is unnecessary. The power of Congress does not extend to the Press."[7]

During the discussion of the Constitution by the States, however, the absence of a guarantee of the freedom of the press was frequently adverted to. Speaking in the South Carolina House of Representatives, Mr. C. C. Pinckney said:

"With regard to the liberty of the press, the discussion of that matter was not forgotten by the members of the Convention. It was fully debated, and the impropriety of saying anything about it in the Constitution clearly evinced.

[4] The Origin and Growth of the American Constitution, p. 230.
[5] Lewis Publishing Co. v. Morgan, 229 U. S. 288 (1913).
[6] Farrand, vol. ii, pp. 334, 341.
[7] Ibid., pp. 617, 618; in Pinckney's plan there was a limitation upon Congress to preserve the freedom of the press. Ibid., vol. iii, pp. 599, 609. A motion was made in the convention to appoint a committee to prepare a bill of rights and was unanimously rejected. Ibid., vol. ii, p. 582.

The general government has no powers but what are expressly granted to it; it therefore has no power to take away the liberty of the press. That invaluable blessing which deserves all the encomiums the gentleman has justly bestowed upon it, is secured by all our state constitutions; and to have it mentioned in our general Constitution would perhaps furnish an argument, hereafter, that the general government had a right to exercise powers not expressly delegated to it."[8]

A different theory was advanced by Hamilton, who, answering the objection that the Constitution contained no bill of rights, and treating specifically the absence of any provision safeguarding the press, asked: "What signifies a declaration that 'the liberty of the press shall be inviolably preserved?' What is the liberty of the press? Who can give it any definition which would not leave the utmost latitude for evasion? I hold it to be impracticable; and from this I infer that its security, whatever fine declarations may be inserted in any Constitution respecting it, must altogether depend upon public opinion, and on the general spirit of the people and of the government. . . ."[9]

---

[8] Farrand, vol. iii, 256; Elliot's Debates, vol. iv, pp. 315, 316. Mr. Pinckney obviously overlooked the possibility that the freedom of the press might incidentally be limited through the exercise by Congress of one of its delegated powers, a possibility which became stronger when the doctrine of implied powers was developed. Particularly was this true in reference to postoffice regulations.

[9] The Federalist, No. 84. In a footnote Hamilton scouts the idea that the liberty of the press may be affected by duties on publications which might be "so high as to amount to a prohibition. . . . We know that newspapers are taxed in Great Britain, and yet it is notorious that the press nowhere enjoys greater liberty than in that country." The extent of duties, if levied, "must depend on legislative discretion, regulated by public opinion. . . . It would be quite as significant to declare that the government ought to be free, that taxes ought not to be excessive, etc., as that the liberty of the press ought not to be restrained." Newspapers were in fact taxed during the Civil War, and revenue to the amount of $980,089 was raised by this means. Lalor, Encyclopaedia of Political Science, (Art., "Press"), vol. iii, 321.

Commenting upon Hamilton's position, Story remarked: "The want of a bill of rights then, is not either an unfounded or illusory objection. The real question is not, whether every sort of right or privilege or claim ought to be affirmed in a constitution; but whether such, as in their own nature are of vital importance, ought not to receive this solemn sanction." Story, Commentaries, vol. iii, p. 721.

A proposal to guarantee the freedom of the press was, however, a part of the plan for a bill of rights which Madison introduced in Congress on June 8, 1789.[10] Such a federal provision had been suggested by the ratifying conventions of three states, and similar provisions were contained in nine state constitutions.[11] Madison's proposal was amended until it provided that "the freedom of speech and of the press . . . shall not be infringed" and its language was further modified until it took the form in which it became a part of the Constitution.

Concerning the meaning of the amendment at the time of its adoption, there has been little, if any controversy, in spite of Hamilton's declaration to the contrary. Blackstone had announced a generally accepted rule when he said that the liberty of the press "consists in laying no *previous* restraint upon publications, and not in freedom from censure for criminal matter when published. Every freeman has an undoubted right to lay what sentiments he pleases before the public; to forbid this, is to destroy the freedom of the press; but if he publishes what is improper, mischievous, or illegal, he must take the consequence of his own temerity. . . . To punish (as the law does at present) any dangerous or offensive writings, which, when published, shall, on a fair and impartial trial be adjudged of a pernicious tendency, is necessary for the preservation of the peace and good order, of government and religion, the only foundations of civil liberty."[12]

In the celebrated case of People v. Croswell, Alexander Hamilton appearing as counsel for the traverser, laid down

[10] Annals of 1st Congress, vol. i, p. 434.

[11] Elliot's Debates, vol. ii, p. 552; vol. iii, 659; Thorpe, Constitutional History, vol. ii, 204.

[12] Cooley's Blackstone, Book iv, pp. 151, 152. Lord Kenyon's view was practically the same. He said: "A man may publish anything which twelve of his countrymen think is not blamable, but he ought to be punished if he publishes what is blamable." Rex v. Cuthill, 27 St. Trials, 675. Cf. Professor Dicey's classic statement: "Freedom of discussion is, then, in England little else than the right to write or say anything which a jury, consisting of twelve shopkeepers, think it expedient should be said or written." Law of the Constitution (8th ed.), p. 242.

the following rule which was unsupported by the English common law, but which has been accepted as a proper definition by a number of the present-day state constitutions. Hamilton said:

"The liberty of the press consists, in my idea, in publishing the truth, from good motives, and for justifiable ends, though it reflect on the government, on magistrates, or individuals. . . . It is essential to say, not only that the measure is bad and deleterious, but to hold up to the people who is the author, that in this our free and elective government, he may be removed from the seat of power."[13] And Story was of the opinion that the guarantee "is neither more nor less, than an expansion of the great doctrine, recently brought into operation in the law of libel, that every man shall be at liberty to publish what is true, with good motives, and for justifiable ends."[14]

The amendment guaranteeing the freedom of the press has never been before the Supreme Court of the United States in such a manner that a comprehensive consideration of its meaning and effect has been entered upon. This is true even of those cases in which the issue was as to the constitutionality of laws denying newspapers the use of the mails for various reasons.[15] In fact, the most important *dictum* of the Supreme Court occurs in a case where a federal law was not involved, the Court adopting Blackstone's definition and holding that "the main purpose of such constitutional provisions is to 'prevent all such *previous restraints* upon publications as had been practised by other governments,' and they do not prevent subsequent punish-

[13] 3 Johns. Cas. (N. Y.) 337 (1798); Hamilton's Works (Lodge's Ed.), vol. vii, p. 339. See the able analysis of Hamilton's definition by Professor Schofield, "Freedom of the Press in the United States," in Proceedings of the American Sociological Society, vol. ix, p. 67, at p. 88 ff. (1915).

[14] Story, Commentaries, vol. iii, p. 732. To the same effect is Kent, Commentaries, vol. ii, lec. 24. A different contention, however, seems to have been made by Tucker, Blackstone's Commentaries, vol. ii, App., Note G, pp. 11–30.

[15] These cases will be considered later in this chapter.

ment of such as may be deemed contrary to the public welfare."[16]

The cases, as well as the text-writers, seem to settle that the first amendment to the Federal Constitution announced no new principles; it must be interpreted in reference to its meaning at common law. The principal inhibition upon the legislature is in the enactment of *previous restraints,* but even here not absolutely. By the civil law of libel, as it was when the Constitution was adopted, the one publishing had to answer for personal wrongs, and the criminal law could punish for defamatory, obscene, blasphemous or seditious libels. To this extent, there could be, and, in fact, were, previous restraints.[17]

But a recent writer, after an able consideration of the early declarations in the light of their history, comes to the

---

[16] Patterson v. Colorado, 205 U. S. 458 (1907). But see Mr. Justice Harlan's dissent, Professor Schofield's criticism of the majority opinion (Freedom of the Press in the United States, pp. 110-112), and Respublica v. Oswald, 1 Dall. 319 (1788). In U. S. v. Cruikshank, 92 U. S. 542 (1876), the court held: "The First Amendment to the Constitution . . . like the other amendments proposed and adopted at the same time, was not intended to limit the powers of the state governments in respect to their own citizens, but to operate upon the national government alone. 'The scope and application of these amendments are no longer subjects of discussion here.' They left the authority of the states just where they found it, and added nothing to the already existing powers of the United States."

Professor Schofield is of the opinion that the Slaughter House Cases, 16 Wall. 36 (1872), are authority for the principle that "the right to publish truth on matters of national public concern is one of the privileges and immunities of citizens of the United States protected from abridgment by any state by the first prohibition in the Fourteenth Amendment." Freedom of the Press in the United States, p. 113. It was held in U. S. v. Hall, 26 Fed. Cas. 79 (1871), that "the right of freedom of speech, and other rights enumerated in the first eight articles of amendment to the Constitution of the United States, are the privileges and immunities of citizens of the United States, that they are secured by the Constitution, that Congress has the power to protect them by appropriate legislation." See Lien, Privileges and Immunities of Citizens of the United States, p. 69. The Supreme Court in Patterson v. Colorado, above, refused to decide whether the liberty of the press declared in the First Amendment, is included by the word "liberty" in the Fourteenth Amendment. These questions, however, are outside the purview of the present discussion.

[17] Patterson, Liberty of the Press, Speech and Public Worship, p. 61 ff.; 2 Willoughby on the Constitution, 844; and Townshend, Slander and Libel, 2d ed., sec. 252.

conclusion that "they obliterated the English common-law test of supposed bad tendency to determine the seditious or blasphemous character of a publication, and hence obliterated the English common-law crimes of sedition and blasphemy; shifted the law of obscene and immoral publications from the region of libel to the region of public nuisance; and left standing only the law of defamatory publications, materially modifying that." Professor Schofield goes on to say that "the declarations wiped out the English common-law rule in criminal prosecutions of defamatory libel, 'The greater the truth the greater the libel,'" and "threw on American judges in civil and criminal actions for defamatory libel the new work of determining what is truth in a publication on a matter of public concern." The correct view, in this author's opinion, is that "if liberty of the press in the First Amendment means anything it legalizes published truth on all matters of public concern."[18] Without, however, attempting to pass judgment on Professor Schofield's criticism of the cases, it will be possible, from either view, to ascertain whether the freedom of the press has ever been abridged by the denial of the use of the mails (for freedom of publication includes, although perhaps not absolutely, freedom of circulation), and to set the limits of congressional action.

Not until 1836 was there any serious discussion of the meaning of the phrase "liberty of the press" and the limitations it might impose upon the postal regulations which Congress had the power to make.[19] But during this year an exhaustive debate took place in the Senate as a result of President Jackson's message (December 2, 1835) urging the enactment of legislation to check the incendiary publications with which the Northern abolitionists were flooding

---

[18] Schofield, Freedom of the Press in the United States, pp. 78, 79 and 110.

[19] The freedom of the press had, of course, figured in the discussion of the so-called Sedition Act passed by Congress on July 14, 1798. It was a factor also in the consideration by the Senate (December, 1901) of legislation "to prevent the teaching and promulgation of anarchical doctrines in the United States." See my paper, "Federal Interference with the Freedom of the Press," 23 Yale Law Journal, 559 and authorities there cited.

the slave states. The evil complained of was serious, and the states were making strenuous objections to the continued presence in the mails of such literature.

On July 29, 1835, for example, the *Southern Patriot* of Charleston, S. C., complained that the mails from the North were "literally overburthened with the newspaper called 'The Emancipator' and two tracts entitled 'The Anti-Slavery Record' and 'The Slaves' Friend.'" This was declared a "monstrous abuse of the public mail" and the publications were denounced as moral poison, the *Patriot* adding: "If the general post office is not at liberty [to prevent circulation], *it is impossible to answer for the security of the mail in this portion of the country*, which contains such poisonous and inflammatory matter."[20] The Charleston postoffice was in fact entered, and this particular consignment of papers destroyed. "Extreme cases require extreme remedies," said the *Patriot*, and the Charleston *Mercury* went so far as to predict that anyone violating the South Carolina law against circulation "would assuredly expiate his offence on the gallows."[21] Practically all of the Southern States had extremely stringent statutes and several provided capital punishment for offenders.[22]

This occurrence at Charleston led Samuel L. Gouverneur, postmaster at New York, to suggest to Amos Kendall, the postmaster general, that the transmission of such papers be suspended, but Arthur Tappan, president of the American Anti-slavery Society, declined to surrender "any rights or privileges which we possess in common with our fellow citizens in regard to the use of the United States mail."[23]

---

[20] Niles' Register, vol. xlviii, p. 402.

[21] Ibid., p. 403.

[22] See Hurd, Law of Freedom and Bondage, vol. ii, 9, 10, 86, 97, 99, 147, 161, 170, 173. The Virginia law specifically included postmasters within its provisions. One indictment under the Alabama law was based upon the following objectionable language: "God commands, and all nature cries out, that man should not be held as property. The system of making men property has plunged 2,250,000 of our fellow countrymen into the deepest physical and moral degradation, and they are every moment sinking deeper." Niles' Register, vol. xlix, p. 358.

[23] Niles' Register, vol. xlviii, p. 447.

Local postmasters nevertheless began to take matters in their own hands. In regard to the detention of incendiary matter by the Charleston postoffice, Kendall wrote:

"I am satisfied that the postmaster general has no legal authority to exclude newspapers from the mail, nor prohibit their carriage or delivery on account of their character or tendency, real or supposed. . . .

"The post office department was created to serve the people of *each* and *all* of the United States and not to be used as the instrument of their *destruction*. . . . Entertaining these views, I cannot sanction and will not condemn the step you have taken. Your justification must be looked for in the character of the papers detained, and the circumstances by which you are surrounded."[24] Kendall left it to the discretion of the local postmasters as to whether they would carry out their official duties, or obey the laws of the local jurisdictions.[25]

It was, therefore, no surprise when Jackson adverted to the situation, and in his annual message asked for legislation denying such publications the facilities of the postoffice. President Jackson wrote:

"I must also invite your attention to the painful excitement produced in the south, by the attempts to circulate, through the mails, inflammatory appeals addressed to the passions of the slaves, in prints, and in various sorts of publications, calculated to stimulate them to insurrection and to produce all the horrors of a servile war. . . .

"In leaving the care of other branches of this interesting subject to the state authorities, to whom they properly belong, it is nevertheless proper for Congress to take such measures as will prevent the post office department, which was designed to foster an amicable intercourse and correspondence between all members of the confederacy, from being used as an instrument of the opposite character. The general government to which the great trust is confided of

[24] Niles' Register, vol. xlviii, p. 448.

[25] The legal aspects of this solution of the problem will be treated in the chapter following.

preserving inviolate the relations created among the states by the Constitution is especially bound to avoid, in its own action, anything that may disturb them. I would, therefore, call the special attention of Congress to the subject, and respectfully suggest the propriety of passing such a law as will prohibit, under severe penalties, the circulation in the southern states, through the mail, of incendiary publications intended to instigate the slaves to insurrection."[26]

On December 21, 1835, Calhoun moved that "so much of the President's message as relates to the transmission of incendiary publications by the United States mail be referred to a special committee." King of Alabama expressed the opinion of several that the regular standing committee on postoffices would do, since he "felt a confident belief that there was no disposition in any of its members to have the public mails prostituted to a set of fanatics." Preston of South Carolina thought that a solution of the evil could be arrived at by a method other than barring the publications from the mail. He proposed "that the depositing of an incendiary publication in the post office should be constituted an offence in the state where it took place, and the letting of it out of the post office should be equally deemed an offence where it occurred."[27] Nevertheless, Calhoun's view prevailed and the message was referred to a select committee of which he was made chairman.[28] An elaborate report written by him was presented to the Senate on February 4, 1836,[29] but with the unqualified concurrence of only one fellow committeeman. The others opposed, either any federal action at all, Calhoun's theory as to the remedy,

[26] Statesman's Manual, vol. ii, p. 911.
[27] 12 Debates of Congress, 26, 33.
[28] Calhoun had for some time been interested in the problem, his attitude being indicated in September, when he wrote to the editor of the Washington *Telegraph:* "The indications are that the south will be unanimous in their resistance and that their resistance will be of the most determined character, even to the extent of disunion; if that should be necessary to arrest the evil. I trust, however, it may be arrested far short of such extremity." Niles' Register, vol. xlix, 49.
[29] 12 Debates of Congress, 383; Calhoun's Works, vol. v, p. 191.

or some of the details of the measure which was recommended.

The committee's report was based upon the premise that Congress had not the power to pass legislation in accordance with the President's recommendation to exclude the objectionable publications from the mails; such a law, Calhoun thought, "would be a violation of one of the most sacred provisions of the Constitution, and subversive of reserved powers essential to the preservation of the domestic institutions of the slaveholding states, and with them, of their peace and security." This would be closely analogous to the Sedition Act which made it a crime to print "any false, scandalous and malicious writing or writings, against the government of the United States," or Congress, or the President, "with intent to defame . . . or to bring them . . . into contempt or disrepute . . . or to incite against them, or either of them, the hatred of the good people of the United States."[30]

But, said Calhoun, postulating the unconstitutionality of these provisions, "as abridging the freedom of the press, *which no one now doubts,* it will not be difficult to show that if, instead of inflicting punishment for publishing, the act had inflicted punishment for circulating through the mails for the same offence, it would have been equally unconstitutional . . . To prohibit circulation, is in effect, to prevent publication . . . each is equally an abridgment of the freedom of the press.

"The prohibition of any publication on the ground of its being immoral, irreligious, or intended to excite rebellion or insurrection, would have been equally unconstitutional; and, from parity of reason, the suppression of their circulation through the mail would be no less so."[31]

The fallacy of this is evident. So far as the Sedition Act is concerned, there are two grounds upon which it could be attacked: lack of congressional power to punish sedition, and abridgment of the freedom of the press. The first

---

[30] 1 Stat. L. 596.
[31] Italics are mine.

question, for present purposes, needs no discussion;[32] but, as for the second, it is well settled that punishment for seditious, obscene, defamatory and blasphemous publications, is not in violation of the freedom of the press.[33] In the United States, then, there is no constitutional restriction which will compel the government impotently to remain the subject of attacks upon its stability. The Act of 1798 was very broad and objectionable on this ground, but the prohibition of seditious utterances urging the use of force or unlawful means to overthrow the government or falsely defamatory of federal officers would not infringe any provision of the bill of rights.[34]

[32] The subject has been given very adequate treatment by Mr. Henry Wolfe Bilké in his paper on "The Jurisdiction of the United States over Seditious Libel," 50 American Law Register, 1. Mr. Bilké says: "The power to punish, for seditious libel, it is submitted, results to the United States, first from its inherent right to adopt such measures as are necessary for its self-preservation, and second, from its right to adopt such measures as are necessary to secure its officers in the due administration of their duties." While it is the better view that Congress has no powers inherent in sovereignty (see 1 Willoughby on the Constitution, 66), the Supreme Court apparently rested its decisions in the Chinese Exclusion Cases [*sub. nom.* Chae Chan Ping v. U. S., 130 U. S. 581 (1888), and especially Fong Yue Ting v. U. S., 149 U. S. 698 (1892)] on a contrary theory. These cases furnish the authority for the first conclusion just quoted, while the case of In Re Neagle, 135 U. S. 1 (1889), is made the basis for the second reason why it is within the power of the United States to punish sedition. At the time of the passage of the act, it had not yet been decided that the federal courts possessed no common law criminal jurisdiction. U. S. v. Hudson & Goodwin, 7 Cranch 32 (1812). The Federalists maintained that such jurisdiction did exist, and that since sedition was a common law offence, Congress could make it statutory and thus aid the courts in its punishment.

[33] Patterson, Liberty of the Press, etc., p. 61. Professor Schofield is of the opinion (Freedom of the Press in the United States, p. 87) that "Liberty of the Press as declared in the First Amendment and the English common-law crime of sedition cannot co-exist"; but certain it is, that without impairing the freedom of the press, Congress may punish seditious utterances counseling the use of force or unlawful means, and falsely defaming public officials.

[34] The weight of authority upholds this view. See Bilké, *op. cit.;* 2 Willoughby on the Constitution, 845; Von Holst (Constitutional History, vol. i, 142) considers the law "unquestionably unconstitutional" and this opinion is supported by 2 Tucker on the Constitution, 669. Story (Commentaries, vol. iii, 744) declines to commit himself, but intimates that the law was valid. The chief objection, as I have said, was to the very broad terms of the act.

But legislation of the character urged by Jackson was not on all fours with the Sedition Act, for by that act the government was punishing publications which it deemed inimical to its own safety. The incendiary matter, however, concerned the states and only a portion of them; the power of Congress to prohibit it, therefore, was doubtful, unless the evil reached such proportions that the menace to the states was a menace to the federal government. To Calhoun it seemed also that the prohibition of circulation through the mails was tantamount to a prohibition of publication.

The right "to determine what papers are incendiary," the report argued, and as such to "prohibit their circulation through the mail, necessarily involves the right to determine what are not incendiary and to enforce their circulation"; both were matters of state prerogative. And, if "consequently the right to protect her internal peace and security belongs to a state, the general government is bound to respect the measures adopted by her for that purpose, and to cooperate in their execution, as far as its delegated powers may admit, or the measure may require. Thus, in the present case, the slaveholding states having the unquestionable right to pass all such laws as may be necessary to maintain the existing relation between master and slave in those states, their right, of course, to prohibit the circulation of any publication or intercourse calculated to disturb or destroy that relation is incontrovertible." The general government is bound, "in conformity to the principle established, to respect the laws of the state in their exercise, and so to modify its act as not only not to violate those of the states, but as far as practicable, to cooperate in their execution."

Simultaneously with the presentation of this report, Calhoun introduced a bill, framed in accordance with his views, making it unlawful for any postmaster to receive and put in the mail any publication addressed to a jurisdiction where its circulation was forbidden. It was made a crime to deliver such prohibited mail to any person not "duly authorized . . . to receive the same" by the local authorities, and there was a further provision that the laws of the United States should not be allowed to protect any postmaster accused of violating local regulations. By this means, Calhoun thought to preserve the liberty of the press and hand the matter over to the states for their settlement.[35]

The constitutional questions involved in the report and law proposed gave rise to a debate of such importance that it has several times been referred to by the Supreme Court of the United States in passing on partially analogous matters.[36] Many different views were advanced as to the correct interpretation of the postal grant which at this time had received practically no consideration by the judiciary. Webster, for example, contended that the proposed law "conflicted with that provision of the Constitution which prohibited Congress from passing any law to abridge the freedom of speech or of the press. What was the liberty of the press?" he asked. "It was the liberty of printing as well as the liberty of publishing, in all the ordinary modes of publication; and was not the circulation of papers through the mails an ordinary mode of publication? . . . Congress might, under this example, be called upon to pass laws to suppress the circulation of political, religious, or any other description of publications which produced excitement in the states." Finally, he argued, "Congress had not the power, drawn from the character of the paper, to decide whether it should be carried in the mail or not; for such decision would be a direct abridgment of the freedom of the press."[37]

Clay argued to the same effect, considering the bill uncalled for by public sentiment, unconstitutional, and containing "a principle of a most dangerous and alarming character."[38] Buchanan's views, however, were different. "It

[35] 12 Debates of Congress, 383. Postmasters were further enjoined "to coöperate, as far as may be, to prevent the circulation of any pamphlet" where it was forbidden by local laws.

[36] Ex parte Jackson and Lewis Publishing Co. v. Morgan.

[37] 12 Debates of Congress, 1721.

[38] Ibid., 1728.

was one thing [he said] not to restrain or punish publications; it was another and an entirely different thing to carry and circulate them after they have been published. The one is merely passive, the other is active. It was one thing to leave our citizens entirely free to print and publish and circulate as they pleased; and it was another thing to call upon us to aid in their circulation. From the prohibition to make any law 'abridging the freedom of speech or of the press,' it could never be inferred that we must provide by law for the circulation through the post office of everything which the press might publish."[39]

Senator Davis of Massachusetts charged, quite properly, it seems to me, that the report and bill were in conflict, since "the report sets forth that Congress has no power to make a law to restrain the circulation of incendiary papers through the mail, because the post masters have no right to determine what is and what is not incendiary; and because to shut papers out of the mail, would be an invasion of the liberty of the press." But the bill would have the United States adopt and enforce state laws prohibiting the circulation of incendiary papers, "having constitutional power so to do and being bound in duty so to do."[40] Another difficulty, as Davis went on to say, was "that incendiary matter is anything unfavorable to slavery. The general principle urged by the Senator from Carolina is, that where the states have power to legislate, the United States is bound to carry into execution their laws. They have the power to prohibit the circulation of incendiary matter, and therefore Congress ought to aid that power."

But to this "there are insurmountable difficulties. How and by whom, is this law to be executed? Who is to de-

[39] 12 Debates of Congress, 1724.

[40] Ibid., 1149. As a matter of fact practically all of the state constitutions contained provisions guaranteeing the freedom of the press. There was, however, liability for abuse in Maine, Connecticut, New York, Pennsylvania, Delaware, Kentucky, Tennessee, Indiana, Illinois, Ohio, Mississippi, Alabama and Missouri. The other constitutions gave unrestricted freedom, subject, of course, to the common law exceptions. See Niles' Register, vol. xlix, 236.

termine, and in what manner, whether the Constitution of Massachusetts, which declares that all men are born free and equal, or the Declaration of Independence . . . touch the subject of slavery or are incendiary? Whoever holds this power may shut up the great channels of inter-communication; may obstruct the great avenues through which intelligence is disseminated."[41]

The use of the mail was declared by Mr. Morris of Ohio to be "a reserved right, with which no law ought to interfere, and not a governmental machine which Congress can withdraw at pleasure or render nugatory by the acts of its officers." Mr. King raised the question as to federal enforcement of circulation in the states against their will. It would depend, he said, on the character of the paper. "If it were a commercial letter . . . or any other paper connected with the granted powers and social relations, as established by the Constitution, and not inconsistent with the reserved rights of the states, in that case its circulation might be enforced. If of a different character it could not be enforced, and the states whose acknowledged rights might be affected, could interfere and arrest the circulation."[42]

This debate, although exhaustive, was inconclusive, and some of the opinions expressed seem, in the light of present day construction of the postal clause, almost absurd. Considerably changed, Calhoun's bill came up for a vote on June 8, 1836, and failed of passage. In its amended form, the bill no longer required that postmasters know the laws of the places to which the mail they received was directed. Under a penalty of being removed from office, they were forbidden to deliver publications, the circulation of which was prohibited by local laws, and in the event that state regulations were not regarded, it was provided that "nothing in the acts

[41] 12 Debates of Congress, 1103.

[42] Ibid., 1124. The House Committee on Postoffices and Post-roads had the President's message under consideration and "came to the conclusion by a vote of 6 to 3, in favor of the constitutionality and expediency of legislation, to restrain the mail circulation of these publications." The majority, however, was unable to agree upon a bill. Ibid., 2944.

of Congress shall be construed" so as to furnish immunity from prosecution.[43]

There is much to be said in favor of this bill as amended. To make their postal agents amenable to local laws as regards the distribution of certain matter is surely within the constitutional power of Congress, and the aim should constantly be for the federal government to legislate so that national and local statutes will be harmonized. "It must be kept in mind," the Supreme Court has said, "that we are one people and that the powers reserved to the states and those conferred on the nation, are adapted to be exercised, whether independently or concurrently, to promote the general welfare, material and moral."[44] In several instances this *dictum* of the Court has been effectuated.

The Judiciary Act of 1789[45] adopted "the laws of the several states" as "rules of decision in trials at common law in courts of the United States in cases where they apply."[46] Quarantine and pilotage regulations have been freely made by the states.[47] During Mr. Jefferson's administration (and this was a precedent relied upon by Calhoun), Congress passed a law forbidding the transportation of free negroes from one state into any other where by local laws they were not permitted to reside.[48] The constitutionality of this act was sustained by Chief Justice Marshall.[49] So also, the congressional act providing for publicity of campaign expenditures forbids any candidate for Representative in Con-

---

[43] 12 Debates of Congress, 1721. The analogy is noticeable between Calhoun's bill and the Webb-Kenyon Act. The purpose of each was substantially the same,—to make state laws more effective. The latter simply excludes from interstate commerce intoxicating liquor intended to be used in violation of the law of destination, providing no penalties, and merely taking from the offender, when the state attempts to punish, his hitherto valid defense that the local authority was interfering with interstate commerce. See my papers, 1 California Law Review, 499 and 28 Harvard Law Review, 225.

[44] Hoke v. U. S., 227 U. S. 308 (1913).

[45] 1 Stat. L. 73.

[46] Golden v. Prince, 10 Fed. Cas. 542 (1814).

[47] Cooley v. Port Wardens, 12 How. 299 (1851).

[48] Act of Feb. 28, 1803; 2 Stat. L. 295.

[49] Brig *Wilson*, 1 Brockenborough, 423 (1820).

gress or for Senator of the United States to "use money in violation of the laws of the state in which he resides,"[50] and Congress has adopted and enforced, as its own, state laws governing elections to the House.[51] Finally, in spite of the constitutional requirement that bankruptcy laws must be uniform, Congress has permitted great variance among the several states, their regulations being enforced by the federal courts. To this there is no constitutional objection.[52]

There is, thus, a considerable body of analogous authority in support of Calhoun's bill as amended. In its first form, the law he proposed was open to objection in that it required deputy postmasters to know the regulations of jurisdictions other than their own, and its effect was to exclude from the mails incendiary matter which the receiving postmaster thought would be considered objectionable at its destination. Under the amended act, however, there would be uniformity, since everything would be transmitted, the restriction being only as to circulation within the states. In administering a great governmental establishment, it should be the aim of Congress not to interfere with the exercise by the states of powers reserved to them.

But Calhoun's argument that the denial of postal facilities was tantamount to a denial of the right of publication, is not well founded, as the Supreme Court of the United States has been at pains to point out; nevertheless it is true that, in some measure at least, the First Amendment insures a use of the postoffice.[53] Whether, if Congress had passed legislation excluding the incendiary literature from the mails, absolutely, the constitutional guarantee of a free press would have been violated, depends upon the character of the publications. If they were of such a seditious tendency that their menace of established institutions in the states was a menace to the federal government, if they fomented dis-

---

[50] Act of August 19, 1911; 37 Stat. L. 25.
[51] Ex parte Siebold, 100 U. S. 371 (1879).
[52] Hanover Bank v. Moyses, 186 U. S. 181 (1902).
[53] Ex parte Jackson, 96 U. S. 727 (1878); see the quotation from this case, below, pp. 115–116.

order and proposed to abolish slavery otherwise than by law, their utterance could have been prohibited, and the denial of postal facilities would have been constitutional. Or, if the objectionable publications did not affect the general government, but incited to arson, murder, etc., and were not simply political appeals, they could have been excluded, and there would have been no infringement of the freedom of the press. But the power of Congress did not extend to the denunciation of anything unfavorable to slavery; freedom of circulation could not be denied publications unless they fell within the limits stated above.

The views expressed in this debate on Calhoun's bill were urged before the Supreme Court of the United States with considerable force when it was called upon to determine the constitutionality of the act excluding lottery tickets from the mails. The prevailing opinion in the senatorial debate had been, as we have seen, that Congress did not possess the power to prohibit the carriage in the mails of the incendiary publications, and to this citation of authority the Supreme Court replied:

"Great reliance is placed by the petitioner upon these views, coming as they did in many instances, from men alike distinguished as jurists and statesmen. But it is evident that they were founded upon the assumption that it is competent for Congress to prohibit the transportation of newspapers and pamphlets over postal routes in any other way than by mail; and of course, it would follow, that if with such a prohibition, the transportation in the mail could also be forbidden, the circulation of the documents would be destroyed and a fatal blow given to the freedom of the press. But we do not think that Congress possesses the power to prevent the transportation in other ways, as merchandise, of matter which it excludes from the mails. To give efficiency to its regulations and prevent rival postal systems, it may, perhaps, prohibit the carriage by others for hire, over postal routes, of articles which legitimately constitute mail matter, in the sense in which those terms were used when the Constitution was adopted,—consisting of letters, and of newspapers and pamphlets, when not sent as merchandise,—but further than this its power of prohibition cannot extend."

And in making a bare denial of the charge that the law abridged the liberty of the press, the Court went on to say:

"In excluding various articles from the mail, the object of Congress has not been to interfere with the freedom of the press, or with any other rights of the people, but to refuse its facilities for the distribution of matter deemed injurious to the public morals. . . .

"Nor can any regulations be enforced against the transportation of printed matter in the mail, which is open to examination, so as to interfere in any manner with the freedom of the press. *Liberty of circulating is as essential to that freedom as liberty of publishing; indeed, without the circulation, the publication would be of little value. If, therefore, printed matter be excluded from the mails, its transportation in any other way cannot be forbidden by Congress.*"[54]

In 1890 Congress extended the inhibition to "any newspaper, circular, pamphlet, or publication of any kind, containing any advertisement of any lottery," and again the Supreme Court held that there had been no impairment of the freedom of the press. The Court said:

"We cannot regard the right to operate a lottery as a fundamental right infringed by the legislation in question; nor are we able to see that Congress can be held, in its enactment, to have abridged the freedom of the press. The circulation of newspapers is not prohibited, but the government declines itself to become an agent in the circulation of printed matter which it regards as injurious to the people. The freedom of communication is not abridged within the intent and meaning of the constitutional provision unless Congress is absolutely destitute of any discretion as to what shall, or shall not be carried in the mails, and compelled

[54] Ex parte Jackson, 96 U. S. 733 (1878); italics are mine.

arbitrarily to assist in the dissemination of matter condemned by its judgment, through the governmental agencies which it controls. That power may be abused furnishes no ground for a denial of its existence, if government is to be maintained at all."[55]

It should be remarked that in these cases the reasoning was largely based on the assumption that prohibiting circulation through the mails was not equivalent to prohibiting publication, and Congress could thus deny postal facilities to matter which it deemed injurious to the people, without interfering with the liberty of the press, since transportation between the states, outside of the mails, would still be possible. But it would seem that this doctrine was repudiated, inferentially at least, when the Supreme Court upheld the law excluding lottery tickets from interstate commerce,[56] and it would, therefore, it seems to me, have been far better if the Court, in the first instance, had adopted other reasoning. It could have held that the liberty of the press suffered abridgment by a denial of postal facilities, but that lottery advertisements, by common opinion, had become as objectionable as immoral writings, and that the latter class,—an exception to the common law guarantee,—could, by reason of a developing moral sense, be made to include the former. Or the Court could have announced as a rule what is probably true, independent of judicial acceptance, that the freedom of the press does not include freedom of advertisement. Or, to advert to the view of Professor Schofield, if the First Amendment protects only publications which have an educational value on matters of national public concern, lottery advertisements do not come within this class; nor do obscene writings.[57] Any one of these theories would have permitted the Supreme Court to render

---

[55] In re Rapier, 143 U. S. 110 (1892); 26 Stat. L. 465.

[56] Champion v. Ames, 188 U. S. 321 (1902). See Goodnow, Social Reform and the Constitution, p. 83, and 2 Willoughby on the Constitution, 741. A flatfooted declaration that the liberty of the press is subject to police regulations concerning what is to be carried in the mails, would, I think, have been justifiable. But the holding of the Jackson case is different.

[57] Schofield, Freedom of the Press in the United States, p. 82.

a logical decision, without putting forth a *dictum* that Congress could not prevent the transportation in other ways of matter excluded from the mails, for this would be a check on circulation which would be a check on publication, and then being forced to take a contrary position in order to declare constitutional a statute which exercised the very power that the Court had doubted. Calhoun's contention, therefore, seems to be the more logical. As it was, the *ratio decidendi* of the Court in the Jackson and Rapier cases would have been impossible had the restraint been against writings of an admittedly innocuous character, against political opinions, for example, or against matters not so universally condemned under the police power. And, to repeat, the Court was forced to deny what, I think, is undoubtedly the better doctrine,—that the liberty of the press may be abridged by restrictions on the use of the mails,—a doctrine that will probably be returned to if Congress legislates on publications that are unobjectionable.

The question of anarchistic publications and the postoffice was raised in March, 1908, when President Roosevelt wrote to Attorney General Bonaparte:

"By my direction the Postmaster General is to exclude *La Questione Sociale,* of Paterson, N. J., from the mails, and it will not be admitted to the mails, unless by order of the court, or unless you advise me that it must be admitted."[58]

In reply to the President's letter, Secretary Bonaparte wrote:

"I am obliged to report that I can find no express provision of law directing the exclusion of such matter from the

[58] 60th Cong., 1st Sess., Senate Doc. No. 426. The paper in question was undoubtedly anarchistic in its tendencies and certain of its sentiments were seditious libels. One editorial, for instance, contained the following:

"Dynamite will help us to win. Two or three of us can deny a regiment of soldiers without fear. . . . Show no sympathy for any soldiers, even if they be sons of the people. As soon as we get hold of the police station, it is our victory. The thing is to kill the entire force. . . . We must get into the armory, and in case we cannot, then we will blow it down with dynamite. . . . We must set fire to three or four buildings in different locations . . . and then start a fire in the center of the city."

mails, or rendering its deposit in the mails an offense against the United States"; but "I have the honor to advise you that it is clearly and fully within the power of Congress to exclude from the mails publications" such as *La Questione Sociale,* "and to make the use, or attempted use, of the mails for the transmission of such writings a crime against the United States."

What Congress thought of anarchy, Mr. Bonaparte said, was shown by the Act of March 7, 1907,[59] excluding and providing for the deportation of anarchists, and the Attorney General made this implied expression of legislative authority (even though in 1903 Congress had expressly refused to pass a law directed against anarchistic publications) a sufficient basis to legalize the action of the President and exclude newspapers which advocated the opinions quoted. The Attorney General's opinion concluded:

"In the absence of any express provision of law or binding adjudication on this precise point, . . . I advise you that, in my opinion, the Postmaster General will be justified in excluding from the mails any issue of any periodical, otherwise entitled to the privileges of second class mail matter, which shall contain any article constituting a seditious libel and counselling such crimes as murder, arson, riot, and treason."

Such action, the opinion said, would be perfectly safe, since "it is well settled that at common law the owner of a libelous picture or placard or document of any kind is entitled to no damages for its destruction in so far at least as its value may depend on its unlawful significance." Hence the federal statutes which provide punishment for postmasters who may "unlawfully detain" or "improperly detain" mailable matter, would not operate.[60]

---

[59] 34 Stat. L. 908.

[60] Rev. Stat. Secs. 3890, 5471. But is this illustration on all fours with the question of illegally excluding *La Questione Sociale?* Mr. Bonaparte mentions the fact that while the article "constitutes a seditious libel and its publication, in my opinion, is undoubtedly a crime at common law," it is not an "offense against the United States in the absence of some federal statute making it one." U. S. v. Hudson & Goodwin, 7 Cranch 32 (1812).

As a matter of fact, the newspaper was excluded for reasons other than its contents, but President Roosevelt transmitted the Attorney General's opinion to Congress and in a special message said:

"Under this opinion I hold that the existing statutes give the President power to prohibit the Postmaster General from being used as an instrument in the commission of crime; that is, to prohibit the use of the mails for the advocacy of murder, arson, and treason; and I shall act upon such construction. Unquestionably, however, there should be further legislation by Congress in this matter. When compared with the suppression of anarchy, every other question sinks into insignificance." Congress has since acted by declaring that the term "indecent" in the section against obscene writings, should include "matter of a character tending to incite arson, murder or assassination."[61]

The Attorney General in his opinion, it may be remarked, did not mention the freedom of the press, and this question was not involved. From what has already been said, it follows that there is no question as to the competency of Congress to pass legislation designed to deny the mails to anarchistic publications if they incite to crime. But the Attorney General's argument as to the power of the President was not well founded; it granted to an administrative officer arbitrary discretion based on no explicit or implied legislative authority, and sanctioned the exercise of this power on the ground that the one injured could have no legal redress. It is, however, simply a question of whether the exclusion was *ultra vires,* not whether it was an abridgment of the freedom of the press.[62]

---

[61] Act of March 4, 1911; 36 Stat. L. 1339.

[62] In U. S. ex rel. Turner v. Williams, 194 U. S. 279 (1904), the Supreme Court held that the provisions of the immigration act of 1903 (32 Stat. L. 1213) for the exclusion and deportation of alien anarchists did not violate any constitutional limitations and that the freedom of the press was not involved. "If the word 'anarchists' should be interpreted as including aliens whose anarchistic views are professed as those of political philosophers innocent of evil

The latest question of the freedom of the press was considered by the Supreme Court in 1913 when it sustained the so-called "newspaper publicity law." This required publications entered as second class matter (with a few exceptions) to furnish the postoffice department with, and publish semi-annually, a sworn statement of their editors and owners, in addition to marking as an advertisement anything for the publication of which, compensation is received. Newspapers were also required to give information as to their circulation figures.[63]

The law was vigorously assailed as being *ultra vires,* as denying due process of law, and as impairing the freedom of the press. It "establishes," said one of the counsel, "a governmental control over newspaper publishers and dictates to them what shall or shall not be published and the manner, form, and time of publishing. In other words, Congress in plain language provided that matter inherently proper and mailable shall be unmailable, not on account of any inherent defect, but solely because the publisher may refuse or neglect to advise the public of certain of his private matters as to which Congress seems to desire the public to be informed. This is not regulation, but paternalism, and a direct and positive abridgment of the freedom of the press."[64]

The Supreme Court, however, by a narrow line of reasoning, sustained the statute, the opinion showing that in order to receive "entry" as second class matter and get the benefit of low rates, the publication must answer a number of questions concerning ownership, editorial supervision, circulation, sample copies, and advertising discrimination. The Court considered the new law as simply laying down additional conditions, compliance with which would enable the publishers to continue "to enjoy great privileges and

intent, . . . in the light of previous decisions, the act, even in this aspect, would not be unconstitutional, as applicable to any alien who is opposed to all organized government."

[63] 37 Stat. L. 553.

[64] Lewis Publishing Company v. Morgan, 229 U. S. 288 (1913). Brief of Morris and Plante, p. 41.

advantages at the public expense." The Court went on to say:

"This being true, the attack on the provision in question as a violation of the Constitution because infringing the freedom of the press and depriving of property without due process of law, rests only upon the illegality of the conditions which the provision exacts in return for the right to enjoy the privileges and advantages of the second class mail classification. The question, therefore, is only this: Are the conditions which were exacted incidental to the power exerted of conferring on the publishers of newspapers, periodicals, etc., the privileges of the second class classification, or are they so beyond the scope of the exercise of that power as to cause the conditions to be repugnant to the Constitution? We may say this is the question, since necessarily if the power exists to legislate by discriminating in favor of the publishers, the right to exercise that power carries with it the authority to do those things which are incidental to the power itself, or which are plainly necessary to make effective the principal authority when exerted."[65]

Whether this reasoning seems convincing or not, it must nevertheless be conceded that legislation to the same effect, not based upon the power of Congress over the mails, would be unconstitutional, and that in this case, Congress has been permitted to do by indirection what it has not the power directly to accomplish. The step is a short one to requiring, for a continuance of the low second class rates, that newspapers print, or refrain from printing, reading matter of a specified character. The decision, however, lends no support to the belief that if this indirect regulation is carried further, or if there is a real interference with the freedom of the press, the Supreme Court will not intervene.

Such are the incidents in which the liberty of the press has figured, and it is difficult to see how it has ever been

---

[65] Lewis Publishing Company v. Morgan, above. Another and more significant phase of this important case is treated in the last chapter of this study.

abridged. The executive order of President Roosevelt excluding *La Questione Sociale* from the mails was *ultra vires,* but, as Attorney General Bonaparte pointed out, the injured parties had slight chance of a remedy at law. Certain it is that the paper in question was so seditious that under a state statute publication could have been stopped, and that an Act of Congress, forbidding such periodicals the privilege of the mails, would not have been in violation of the First Amendment.

The decisions of the Supreme Court which have been quoted lead to no conclusion other than that any attempt on the part of Congress to place a previous restraint upon the press, or even to deny it postal facilities, for no discernible reason, would receive a judicial veto. The exclusion of lottery tickets, obscene matter, and other writings inimical to the public morals, has been clearly within the power of Congress, and legislation forbidding seditious and anarchistic publications when directed against the federal government, or banning them from the mails, would be constitutional. It is true that the "newspaper publicity law," strictly speaking, is a previous restraint, but the Supreme Court considered it as merely laying down additional and reasonable conditions, compliance with which would enable periodical publications to continue to enjoy great and exclusive advantages of second class privileges,—a satisfactory, if not conclusive basis for the decision; as interpreted by the Court, the act promotes, rather than abridges, the liberty of the press.

Neither reason nor precedent justifies the view, eloquently urged by counsel in this case, that Congress by the law exercises "a governmental control over newspaper publishers and dictates to them what shall not be published, and the manner, form, and time of publishing." On the contrary, that great "palladium of liberty,"—the freedom of the press,—seems to be in no danger of demolition through congressional action.

Unreasonable Searches and Seizures.—As with the freedom of the press, the Supreme Court of the United States has rarely been asked to restrain the postal power under the provision of the Fourth Amendment to the Constitution which declares that "the right of the people to be secure in their persons, houses, papers, and effects against unreasonable searches and seizures, shall not be violated, and no warrants shall issue, but upon probable cause, supported by oath or affirmation, and particularly describing the place to be searched, and the persons or things to be seized."[66] The scope of this limitation, as applied to the mails, has been described by the Supreme Court in the following terms:

"A distinction is to be made between different kinds of mail matter, between what is intended to be kept free from inspection, such as letters and sealed packages, subject to letter postage, and what is open to inspection. . . . Letters and sealed packages of this kind in the mail are to be as fully guarded from examination and inspection, except as to their outward form and weight, as if they were retained by the parties forwarding them in their own domiciles. The constitutional guaranty of the right of the people to be secure in their papers against unreasonable searches and seizures extends to their papers thus closed against inspection, wherever they may be. Whilst in the mail, they can only be opened and examined under like warrant, issued upon similar oath or affirmation, particularly in describing the thing to be seized, as is required when papers are subjected to search in one's own household. No law of Congress can place in the hands of officials connected with the postal service any authority to invade the secrecy of letters and such sealed packages; and all regulations adopted as to mail matter of this kind must be in subordination to the

[66] For an historical consideration of this amendment, see Boyd v. U. S., 116 U. S. 616 (1886). See also May, Constitutional History of England, vol. ii, p. 245 ff.; Cooley's Blackstone, Book iv, p. 290 ff.; Annals of 1st Congress, vol. i, pp. 434, 754, and Story, Commentaries, vol. iii, p. 748. Discussions of the general scope of the provision are to be found in 2 Willoughby on the Constitution, 828; Cooley, Constitutional Limitations (7th ed.), p. 429, and Bruce, "Arbitrary Searches and Seizures as Applied to Modern Industry." Green Bag, vol. xviii, p. 273.

great principle embodied in the Fourth Amendment of the Constitution."[67]

The limitation operates chiefly upon administrative officials who attempt to get evidence of violations of the law regarding obscene literature and fraudulent matter excluded from the mails. In regard to this the Court said:

"Whilst regulations excluding matter from the mails cannot be enforced in a way which would require or permit an examination into letters, or sealed packages subject to letter postage, without warrant issued upon oath or affirmation, in the search for prohibited matter, they may be enforced upon competent evidence of their violation obtained in other ways; as from parties receiving the letters and packages, or from agents depositing them in the postoffices, or others cognizant of the facts. And as to the objectionable printed matter which is open to examination, the regulations may be enforced in a similar way, by the imposition of penalties for their violation through the courts, and, in some cases by the direct action of the officers of the postal service. In many instances those officers can act upon their own inspection, and, from the nature of the case, must act without other proof; as where the postage is not prepaid, or where there is an excess of weight over the amount prescribed, or where the object is exposed, and shows unmistakably that it is prohibited, as in the case of an obscene picture or print. In such cases, no difficulty arises, and no principle is violated in excluding the prohibited articles and refusing to forward them. The evidence respecting them is seen by everyone and is in its nature conclusive."[68]

This view of the law has been acquiesced in by Congress which has provided that nothing in the acts excluding certain matters from the mails, "shall be so construed as to authorize any person other than an employee of the Dead Letter Office, duly authorized thereto, to open any letter not addressed to himself."[69] The regulations promulgated

---

[67] Ex parte Jackson, 96 U. S. 727 (1878).
[68] Ibid. But see Hoover v. McChesney, 81 Fed. Rep. 472 (1897).
[69] 25 Stat. L. 873.

for the postoffice department, provide, moreover, that neither postmasters, inspectors, employees, nor officers of the law, "without legal warrant therefor, have authority to open under any pretext a sealed letter while in the mails, not even though it may contain improper or criminal matter, or furnish evidence for the conviction of offenders," and out of excess of caution, it is further added that "the seal of letters or packages suspected to contain unmailable matter shall not be broken to ascertain that fact."[70] The regulations provide that matter manifestly unmailable shall be withdrawn and sent to the Division of Dead Letters with a statement of the facts upon which such action was taken; if there is doubt as to the propriety of such disposition, the matter shall be sent to the Assistant Attorney General for the Postoffice Department, for his decision.[71] Any unlawful opening of the mail by a postal employee is dealt with criminally.[72] Special regulations govern the examination by a customs officer of sealed packages supposed to be dutiable, in the presence of the addressee, but before delivery to him.[73]

If, then, at times, administrative zeal may lead to a disregard of these regulations, the official is criminally liable, and the one whose sealed mail is searched, has a right of action for damages. But the avowed purpose of Congress and of the postoffice department is to subordinate efficiency in the detection of wrongdoing to the right of the people, under the Fourth Amendment, to be secure in their sealed papers when they are in the hands of the government for transmission through the mails.[74]

---

[70] Postal Laws and Regulations of 1913, p. 300.
[71] Ibid., p. 313.
[72] 35 Stat. L. 1125.
[73] Postal Laws and Regulations of 1913, p. 372 ff.
[74] A third limitation on the postal power, namely, due process of law, is most properly treated in the concluding chapter of this essay.

CHAPTER V

The Power of the States to Interfere with the Mails

In the disputed zone between federal authority and the reserved rights of the states, interesting and often acute problems have, of course, frequently developed. The most important of these have probably been with regard to the national control of interstate commerce and the police power of the states, and several times Congress has passed legislation designed to leave certain subjects within the jurisdiction of the states or to make local regulations more effective. In Jefferson's administration, for example, Congress passed a law prohibiting the transportation of free negroes from one state into another where by local laws they were not permitted to reside;[1] the sale of oleomargarine has been made subject to local regulations;[2] Congress has forbidden the transportation of game killed in violation of state laws,[3] and has twice enacted legislation to enable the states more effectively to regulate the sale of intoxicating liquors.[4] Such action has been necessary since congressional silence has been interpreted by the courts as meaning that commerce between the states shall be free, just as, when Congress has acted affirmatively, state laws in conflict are thereby suspended: in both cases the supremacy of the federal authority is unquestioned. Nevertheless local jurisdictions have been permitted to exercise a slight measure of police control.[5]

It would seem evident, at first glance, that, inherently,

---

[1] Act of February 28, 1803, 2 Stat. L. 295; Brig *Wilson*, 1 Brockenborough 423 (1820).

[2] 32 Stat. L. 193; U. S. v. Green, 137 Fed. Rep. 179 (1905).

[3] Criminal Code, sec. 242; Rupert v. U. S., 181 Fed. Rep. 87 (1910).

[4] Act of August 8, 1890, 26 Stat. L. 313 (Wilson Act); Act of March 1, 1913, 37 Stat. L. 699 (Webb-Kenyon Act).

[5] See 2 Willoughby, ch. xlii, and cases there cited.

the power of Congress over the postal system is even more paramount than that over interstate commerce, but there has been practically no judicial determination of the subject, and as there are only a few incidents in which a conflict of jurisdiction has taken place, conclusions as to the exclusiveness of the federal power must be largely speculative. Some aid, it is true, may be drawn from the analogy of interstate commerce, but there is the fundamental difference that postal facilities are established and conducted, while trade between the states is simply regulated, by Congress. From this arises the presumption that the mails are less subject to interference than is interstate trade. Has this in fact proved to be the case?[6]

The first question as to the rights of the states was raised in 1812, when the general assembly of the Presbyterian Church and the Synod of Pittsburgh memorialized Congress to suspend the carrying and opening of the mails on Sunday, but, owing to the "peculiar crisis of the United States" then pending, the petitions were withdrawn and the House Committee on the Postoffice and Postroads did not consider the requests on their merits.[7] In practice the activities were lessened, offices at which the mail arrived on Sunday being kept open for one hour only, and that not during the time of public worship. So, the Senate Committee to which similar memorials were referred, deemed it inexpedient to make any change, particularly "considering the condition of the country, engaged in war, rendering frequent communication through the whole extent of it absolutely necessary."[8]

The practice to which objection was made had obtained since the adoption of the Constitution. By the postal act passed in 1810[9] it was made a duty of postmasters "at all

[6] There is also the question of state power over postroads, but this has been treated in Chapter III, above, p. 82 ff.

[7] Miscellaneous State Papers, vol. ii (American State Papers, vol. xxi), p. 194.

[8] American State Papers (Postoffice), vol. xv, p. 47.

[9] 2 Stat. L. 592.

reasonable hours, on every day of the week, to deliver" mail to the proper persons, and since this provision was reenacted in 1825[10] protests were still received from a number of the states in which rigorous Sunday observance laws had been passed. Upon the memorials which were presented in 1829 the Senate Committee acted unfavorably, but the House Committee acceded so far as to propose the discontinuance of delivery, but the maintenance of transportation;[11] the chief objection seemed to be to the keeping open of the postoffices and not to the carrying of the mails, for which, it was realized, the greatest possible expedition was desirable. In 1830 counter memorials opposed "the interference of Congress upon the ground that it would be legislating upon a religious subject and therefore unconstitutional,"[12] but this argument is clearly untenable, since Sunday legislation has uniformly been upheld, not upon religious grounds, but as a valid exercise of the police power,[13] and Congress certainly has analogous authority so far as concerns the conduct of government business.

During the whole of this period, however, when certain localities and religious bodies desired observance of Sunday by the postoffice, the authority of Congress to make such regulations as it might see fit for the transportation of the mails, was not seriously questioned, and the states did not attempt, under their police power, themselves to take affirmative action. One of the committee reports suggested, but did not argue, a contrary proposition when it asked: "If the arm of the government be necessary to compel respect and obey the laws of God, do not the state governments possess infinitely more power in this respect?" But this implication of authority in the states to interfere with the postal function is later denied when the committee says that

[10] 4 Stat. L. 102.

[11] American State Papers (Postoffice), vol. xv, p. 211. For the lengthy memorials presented, see ibid., pp. 229-241.

[12] Ibid., p. 231.

[13] Freund, Police Power, p. 168 ff.

in order to insure effective Sabbath observance it should be made a crime to receive, write, or read letters.[14] Congress, however, is the sole judge of the primary question. As a House Committee said in 1817: "The power 'to establish postoffices and postroads' is by the Constitution of the United States exclusively tested in Congress; and the transportation and distribution of the mail, at such times and under such circumstances as the public interest may require, are necessarily incident to that power."[15]

It should be remembered, however, that the law provided for delivery "at all reasonable hours, on every day of the week," and so the question is different from that decided by the Supreme Court of the United States in Hennington v. Georgia,[16] where it was held that a state statute prohibiting the running of freight trains on Sunday was, in the absence of congressional regulation of the subject, not invalid as interfering with interstate commerce. But even if Congress had not provided for the carriage of the mails on Sunday, there could be no stoppage under a state statute, since the subject is one for exclusive federal regulation; and if the freight trains in the Georgia case had carried mails, the decision would have been otherwise.

Similarly, the state laws which provide punishment for working on Sunday are inoperative as applied to postal employees (in discharge of their duty imposed by federal regulations) even though the local statute may make no express exception. The question has rarely come before the courts, but it has been held a work of necessity to shoe

---

[14] American State Papers (Postoffice), vol. xv, p. 230. See an interesting article on this subject in the North American Review, July, 1830.

[15] American State Papers (Postoffice), vol. xv, p. 358.

[16] 163 U. S. 299 (1896). ". . . legislative enactments of the states passed under their admitted police power, and having a real relation to the domestic peace, order, health and safety of their people, but which, by their necessary operation, affect to some extent, or for a limited time, the conduct of commerce among the states, are yet not invalid by force alone of the grant of power to Congress to regulate such commerce, if not obnoxious to some other constitutional provision or destructive of some right secured by fundamental law. . . ."

horses used by a stage company in transporting the mail.[17] The work done by postal employees would, therefore, be necessary within the exemption made by nearly all Sunday observance laws; but if this were not the case, the laws would not apply.

Closely allied to this question is that of how far the states may go in making police regulations, regard for which will result in a temporary delay of the mails. As early as 1817 it was held by a federal circuit court that a municipal corporation is competent to prevent the reckless driving of a mail carrier through crowded streets.[18] Of similar import was the advice given the postoffice department in 1852 by Attorney General Crittenden, that municipal ordinances prohibiting railroad trains from running at a rate of more than six miles an hour within the town limits, the mails thereby being delayed, were valid regulations and not in conflict with the act of Congress.

"When such regulations," said the opinion, "are fairly and discreetly made with intent to preserve the peace, safety and well being of the inhabitants of the city, they may be said to flow from powers necessary and proper in themselves, which the act of Congress does not intend to take away or impugn."[19]

---

[17] Nelson v. State, 25 Texas App. 599 (1888). In some states express exemptions are made for the transportation of the mail. Cf. State v. Norfolk & W. R. Co., 33 W. Va. 440 (1890). A typical Sunday observance statute is the following: "No person whatsoever shall work or do any bodily labor on the Lord's day, commonly called Sunday; and no person having children or servants shall command, or wittingly or willingly suffer any of them to do any manner of work or labor on the Lord's day (works of necessity and charity always excepted)" (Public General Laws of Maryland (ed. of 1904), art. xxvii, sec. 384). The general proposition that the state regulations do not apply to postal employees is supported by Commonwealth v. Knox, 6 Mass. 76 (1809), which held that it is not an indictable offence for a carrier of the mail to travel on Sunday. This exemption was not applied to passengers, "nor may he [the carrier] blow his horn to the disturbance of serious people." An indictment did lie, however, against the chief justice of Massachusetts and his associates for travelling on Sunday (1793). See "Sunday Laws," in 2 American Law Review, 226.

[18] U. S. v. Hart, 1 Peters' C. C. 390 (1817).

[19] 5 Opinions of the Attorneys General, 554 (1852).

At later dates the validity of similar regulations requiring trains to stop at particular points was passed upon by the United States Supreme Court and the exercise of local authority was, in several cases, declared inoperative, primarily upon the ground that it interfered with the freedom of trade between the states, and the commercial, rather than the postal, power was relied upon, as in federal incorporation, to furnish the basis of the court's decisions. But the fact that, in many instances, the trains carried the mails under contracts which required expedition was incidentally referred to as a further reason for declaring local regulations invalid.

Thus, when an Illinois statute required an interstate train to turn aside from the direct route for a stop at a station three and one half miles away, the Supreme Court held the requirement to be "an unconstitutional hindrance and obstruction of interstate commerce and of the passage of the mails of the United States. . . .

"It may well be, as held by the courts of Illinois, that the arrangements made by the company with the Postoffice Department of the United States cannot have the effect of abrogating a reasonable police regulation of the state. But a statute of the state, which unnecessarily interferes with the speedy and uninterrupted carriage of the mails of the United States, cannot be considered as a reasonable police regulation."[20] And in a later case the court said:

"The fact that the company has contracts to transport the mails of the United States within a time which requires great speed for the trains carrying them, while not conclusive, may still be considered upon the general question of stopping such trains at certain stations within the boundaries of a state. The railroad has been recognized by Congress and is the recipient of large land grants, and the carrying of the mails is a most important function of such

[20] Illinois Central R. Co. v. Illinois, 163 U. S. 142 (1896). See also 143 Ill. 434; 19 L. R. A. 119 (1892).

a road."[21] The test as laid down by the United States Supreme Court is, therefore, simply one of reasonableness and necessity; and the courts, not the legislatures, are to determine the question.

But there are many cases in which the problem is not so simple, and where the state regulations are so important that their violation should not be permitted under the cloak of federal sanction. Particularly is this true where the detention of a postal empolyee is, superficially, forbidden under the federal statutes, and there arises the dilemma that either the governmental agent is immune from interference while in discharge of his duties and at all times for acts committed in the course of his employment, or that the national regulations must give way.

For example, from the beginning of congressional activity under the postal power, there has constantly been a prohibition, under severe penalties, of any obstruction of the mail. The federal district court for Maryland considered a case where stage horses upon which an innkeeper had a lien were stopped in the public highway while driving a coach containing the mail. The court held that since the United States could not be sued, "the defendant could not justify the stopping of the mail on principles of common law, as they apply to individuals and to the government." But, further, the defendant was not justifiable under the act of Congress which introduced no exception. "Whether the acts which it prohibits to be done were lawful or unlawful before the operation of that law, or independent of it, might or might not be justified, is not material. This law does not allow any justification of a *wilful and voluntary* act of obstruction to the passage of the mail. If, therefore, courts or juries were to introduce exceptions not found in the law itself, by admitting justifications for the breach of the act, which justifications the act does not allow to be made, it would be an assumption of legislative power."[22]

---

[21] Mississippi R. Commission v. Illinois C. R. Co., 203 U. S. 335 (1906). See also Atlantic Coast Line R. Co. v. Wharton, 207 U. S. 328 (1907).

[22] U. S. v. Barney, 3 Hughes' Reports (U. S. C. C.) 545 (1810).

And when a warrant in a civil suit was served on a mail carrier and he was detained thereby, Chief Justice Taney (on circuit) held that the warrant was not justification to the traverser, a constable, yet the mere *serving* "would not render the party liable, to an indictment under this law. But if, by serving the warrant, he *detained* the carrier, he would then be liable."[23] Here also the immunity was simply as to civil proceedings.

But when a carrier, while discharging his duty, was arrested upon an indictment for murder, and it was argued that this was an obstruction of the mail within the federal statute, the Supreme Court refused to listen to the plea, and held that the law, "by its terms applies only to persons who 'knowingly and wilfully' obstruct the passage of the mail or of its carrier; that is, to those who know that the acts performed will have that effect and perform them with the intention that such shall be their operation. When the acts which create the obstruction are in themselves unlawful, the intention to obstruct will be imputed to their author, although the attainment of other ends may have been his primary object. The statute has no reference to acts lawful in themselves, from the execution of which a temporary delay to the mails unavoidably follows. All persons in the public service are exempt, as a matter of public policy, from arrest upon a civil process while thus engaged. Process of that kind can, therefore, furnish no justification for the arrest of a carrier of the mail. . . . The rule is different when the process is issued upon a charge of felony. No officer or employee of the United States is placed by his position, or the services he is called to perform, above responsibility to the legal tribunals of the country, and to the ordinary processes for his arrest and detention when accused of a felony, in the forms prescribed by the Constitution and laws.

"The public inconvenience which may occasionally follow from the temporary delay in the transmission of the mail

[23] U. S. v. Harvey, 8 Law Reporter, 77 (U. S. C. C., 1845).

caused by the arrest of its carriers on such charges is far less than that which would arise from extending to them the immunity for which the counsel of the government contends. Indeed, it may be doubted whether it is competent for Congress to exempt the employees of the United States from arrest on criminal process from the state courts when the crimes charged against them are not merely *mala prohibita* but are *mala in se*. But whether such legislation of that character be constitutional or not, no intention to extend such exemption should be attributed to Congress unless clearly manifested by its language."[24]

Thus, the Supreme Court of Maine decided that a mail carrier, while in the performance of his duties, is liable to arrest for an offense against the law of the state, even though it be not a felony but a violation of a liquor regulation, and the public employment of the carrier will not justify him in assaulting the officer who serves the warrant.[25] It was held, further, that preventing a horse from being taken from the stable for the purpose of carrying the mail was no offense under the federal law since the mail had to be *in transitu*.[26]

The attachment, knowingly, of a coach carrying the mail is void, being an obstruction;[27] but levy on and sale of a ferryboat used to carry the mail do not constitute an obstruction.[28] In United States v. De Mott[29] it was held that the statute "is applicable to a person stopping a train carrying the United States mail, although he has obtained a judgment and writ of possession from a state court against the railroad company in respect to lands about to be crossed by such train." It is, moreover, not a sufficient plea to an

---

[24] U. S. v. Kirby, 7 Wall. 482 (1869); see also U. S. v. Clark, 23 Int. Rev. Rec. 306 (U. S. D. C., 1877).

[25] Penny v. Walker, 64 Maine 430 (1874).

[26] U. S. v. McCracken, 3 Hughes' Reports (U. S. C. C.) 544 (1878).

[27] Harmon v. Moore, 59 Me. 428 (1871).

[28] Lathrop v. Middleton, 23 Cal. 257 (1863). In this case, however, the boat was at the time in an unfinished condition and had not been used on the ferry.

[29] 3 Fed. Rep. 478 (1880).

indictment for obstructing the mails, that the defendant was required by state law to collect tolls in advance from all drivers of wagons. "It is not the right of the company to the tolls under the state law which is doubted," said the Court, "but the right to stop the passage of the mails to enforce their collection which is denied."[30]

The rule may thus be stated to be as follows: In order to guard against obstruction of the mails, postoffice employees, while in discharge of their duty, have immunity from interference on civil processes, but are liable for felonies, and perhaps, misdemeanors. But a different and more serious question upon which these cases throw little or no light, is presented when a postal agent in the discharge of a duty imposed by federal law (neglect of duty being punishable) thereby performs an act which has been made criminal by the state.[31] There are, naturally, but few cases when this conflict arises, but it is entirely possible, perhaps the most favorable opportunity being when a postmaster distributes certain mail matter, the possession or dissemination of which the state has declared unlawful. This conflict was once presented very acutely.

In the senatorial debate on Calhoun's bill to deal with incendiary publications in the mails, the federal question

[30] United States v. Sears, 55 Fed. Rep. 268 (1893). In Turnpike Co. v. Newland, 15 N. C. 463 (1834), it was held that a mail coach was a "pleasure carriage" within the meaning of the local statute imposing tolls for the use of the road. The use of state facilities by persons employed in the federal civil service, said the court, "must be deemed intended to be on the terms prescribed to all persons, unless the law under which it is performed declared the contrary. We have found no act of Congress exempting persons or carriages engaged in the business of the postoffice from the payment of tolls for passing ferries, bridges or roads." Payment was, therefore, required.

[31] The seriousness of this conflict was well expressed by Chief Justice Marshall in Cohens v. Virginia, 6 Wheaton 264 (1821). "To interfere with the penal laws of a state," he said, "where they are not levelled against the legitimate powers of the Union, but have for their sole object the internal government of the country, is a very serious measure which Congress cannot be disposed to adopt lightly or inconsiderately. The motives for it must be serious and weighty. It would then be taken deliberately and the intention would be clearly and unequivocally expressed."

of interference with the freedom of the press received the greatest attention[32] and the equally important question of the validity of state legislation was only meagrely considered. Nearly all of the Southern States had extremely stringent laws, making the publication, circulation and even the possession of objectionable literature punishable by severe penalties. Postal officials were not exempted; in Virginia they were specifically included.[33] Nevertheless, the objectionable dissemination continued, and Amos Kendall, postmaster general, who had left the problem largely in the hands of local officers,[34] was importuned from many sources to take decisive action. The citizens of Petersburg, Va., on August 8, 1835, petitioned him to "adopt such lawful regulations in his department as may be calculated to prevent" the dissemination of incendiary papers. More elaborate resolutions were adopted at Richmond, and at Charleston it was declared:

"That the postoffice establishment cannot consistently with the Constitution of the United States and the objects of such an institution, be converted into an instrument for the dissemination of incendiary publications, and that it is the duty of the federal government to provide that it shall not be so prostituted, which can easily be effected by merely making it unlawful to transport by the public mail, through the limits of any state, any seditious papers, forbidden by the laws of such state, to be introduced or circulated therein, and by adopting the necessary regulations to effect the object." The resolutions then went on to assert "the right of each state to provide by law against the introduction of a *moral pestilence,* calculated to endanger its existence, and to give authority to their (*sic*) courts adequate to the suppression of the evil."[35]

---

[32] See above, Chapter IV.

[33] Hurd, Law of Freedom and Bondage, vol. ii, pp. 9, 10.

[34] See above, p. 105.

[35] Niles' Register, vol. xlviii, p. 446. The Richmond resolutions were less elaborate, simply requesting the postmaster general "to use all powers vested in him by law" to prevent the dissemination and delivery of the objectionable matter.

To the Petersburg resolutions, Kendall replied at some length, very conciliatingly, and pleaded that the discretion was not vested in him. "Having no official right to decide upon the character of papers passing through the mails," he said, "it is not within my power by any 'lawful regulation' to obviate the evil of which the citizens of Petersburg complain. If any necessity exists for a supervision over the productions of the press which are transmitted by mail, all will agree that it ought not to be vested in the head of the executive department. . . .

"For the present I perceive no means of relief except in the responsibilities voluntarily assumed by the postmasters through whose offices the seditious matter passes."[36]

In a letter to Gouverneur, the postmaster at New York, who had exercised his discretion in detaining certain publications, Kendall expressed the same views but argued the constitutional problems at greater length. "As a measure of great public necessity," he said, "you and the other postmasters who have assumed the responsibility of stopping these inflammatory papers, will, I have no doubt, stand justified in that step before your country and all mankind." Perhaps also, he suggested, the abolitionists did not have their imagined clear legal right to the use of the mails for distributing insurrectionary papers. When the states became independent, he argued, "they acquired a right to prohibit the circulation of such papers within their territories; and their power over the subject of slavery and its incidents was in no degree diminished by the adoption of the federal Constitution. . . .

"Now," he asked, "have these people a legal right to do by the mail carriers and postmasters of the United States, acts, which, if done by themselves or their agents, would lawfully subject them to the punishment due felons of the deepest dye? Are the officers of the United States compelled by the Constitution and laws to become the instruments and accomplices of those who design to baffle and

[36] Niles' Register, vol. xlix, p. 7.

make nugatory the constitutional laws of the states,—to fill them with sedition, murder, insurrection,—to overthrow those institutions which are recognized and guaranteed by the Constitution itself?

"And is it entirely certain that any existing law of the United States would protect mail carriers and postmasters against the penalties of the state laws, if they shall knowingly carry, distribute or hand out any of these forbidden papers? . . . It might be vain for them to plead that the postoffice law made it their clear duty to deliver all papers which came by mail. In reply to this argument, it might be alleged, that the postoffice imposes penalties on postmasters for '*improperly*' detaining papers which come by the mail; and that the detention of the papers in question is not improper because their circulation is prohibited by valid state laws. Ascending to a higher principle, it might be plausibly alleged, that no law of the United States can protect from punishment any man, whether a public officer or citizen, in a commission of an act which the state, acting within the undoubted sphere of her reserved rights has declared to be a crime.

"Every citizen may use the mail for any lawful purpose. The abolitionists may have a legal right to its use for distributing their papers in New York, where it is lawful to distribute them, but it does not follow that they have a legal right to that privilege for such a purpose in Louisiana or Georgia where it is unlawful."[37] Arguing in this manner, Kendall arrived at his conclusion that the postmasters should use their own judgment and act on their own responsibility.

The postmaster general's letter has been so fully set forth because it presents, although it by no means solves, all the constitutional questions to which this situation gave rise. The disputed issues were destined never to come before the Supreme Court of the United States for a judicial consideration; they were, however, to be meagrely discussed on the floor of the Senate and twenty years later were to be passed

[37] Niles' Register, vol. xlix, p. 9.

upon by the Attorney General in an official opinion. Was the Virginia law, including postal officials, constitutional? Could they be punished for receiving and circulating the prohibited matter when to do so was required by federal law as a part of their official duty? Could a citizen of the state be punished for receiving mail of a certain character? Were the states competent to exclude from their borders publications calculated to stir up disaffection among the slave population?

Attorney General Caleb Cushing was called upon, in 1857, to pass upon some of these questions. The facts of the particular case presented to him were these: The postmaster of Yazoo City refused to deliver a newspaper for the "alleged cause that the same contained matter of which the tendency and object were to produce disaffection, disorder and rebellion among the colored population of the state of Mississippi; and that the delivery of the same by him would constitute a penitentiary crime according to the laws of that state." The removal of the postmaster for malfeasance in office was requested since the act of July 2, 1836, provided punishment for postmasters who unlawfully detained the mail. On the other hand, the laws of Mississippi made it a crime, punishable by not more than ten years' imprisonment, to bring into the state or circulate any printed matter "calculated to produce disaffection among the slave population."[38]

Cushing declared the postal power to be "conferred in very imperfect terms." The clause in the Constitution, he said, provides "for a means or incident without providing for the principal or end. Still we may take it for granted here, that, by this phrase, the states designed to communicate the entire mail power to the United States." But, on the other hand, it is indisputable that "each state has, and must have, jurisdiction as regards the matter of insurrection or treason. To deny this would be to deny to the in-

[38] 8 Opinions of the Attorneys General, 489 (1857); 5 Stat. L. 80.

habitants of a state the power of self preservation, . . . a right inalienable and imprescriptible."

With this and the completeness of congressional power over the mails as premises, Cushing said the question was as follows: "Has a citizen of one of the United States plenary, indisputable right to employ the functions and the officers of the Union as the means of enabling him to produce insurrection in another of the United States? Can the officers of the Union lawfully lend its functions to the citizens of one of the states for the purpose of promoting insurrection in another state?

"It is obvious to say that, inasmuch as it is the constitutional obligation of the United States to protect each of the states against 'domestic violence' and to make provisions to 'suppress insurrection'" it cannot be the right or duty of the United States or any of its officers "to promote, or be the instrument of promoting, insurrection in any part of the United States."[39]

Reasoning thus, Cushing concludes "that a deputy postmaster or other citizen of the United States is not required by law to become, knowingly, the enforced agent or instrument of enemies of the public peace, to disseminate, in their behalf, within the limits of any one of the states of the Union, printed matter, the design and tendency of which are to promote insurrection in such state." But at the outset, he said, any settlement of the particular case is involved in "a preliminary question of unsettled fact. The question is whether the contents of the particular newspaper had for their tendency and object to incite insurrection in the state of Mississippi." There are questions also as to the private rights of the addressee and the penal obligations of the deputy postmaster. These are for the courts. They only can "determine the question of the deputy postmaster's

---

[39] Mr. Cushing argued (p. 494) that "it cannot be unlawful to detain that which it is unlawful to deliver." But the word "unlawful" in the congressional statute is not to be construed according to state regulations. Whether the detention of the mail is sanctioned must be determined by state standards.

penal liability, whether on the side of the United States or of the state of Mississippi." The attorney general thus comes to no absolutely definite conclusion, but the implication is very strong that there is no federal immunity from prosecution under the state law, and, conversely, that there can be no prosecution under federal law for neglect of duty or malfeasance.

To the same effect, but more clear cut, was the opinion of John Randolph Tucker sent to Governor Wise of Virginia on November 26, 1859.[40] The laws of Virginia provided that "if a postmaster or deputy postmaster know that any such book or writing [inciting the negroes to rebellion] has been received at his office in the mail, he shall give notice thereof to some justice, who shall inquire into the circumstances and have such book or writing burned in his presence; if it appears to him that the person to whom it is directed subscribed therefor, knowing its character, or agreed to receive it for circulation to aid the purposes of the abolitionists the justice shall commit such person to jail. If any postmaster or deputy postmaster violate this section, he shall be fined not exceeding $200."

In his opinion, Tucker, as attorney general of the state, held the law to be entirely constitutional. It does not, he said, "properly considered, conflict with federal authority in the establishment of postoffices and postroads. This federal power to transmit and carry mail matter does not carry with it the power to publish or circulate. . . .

"With the transmission of the mail matter to the point of its reception the federal power ceases. At that point the power of the state becomes exclusive. Whether her citizens shall receive the mail matter is a question exclusively for her determination. . . .

"It is true that the postmaster is an officer of the federal government; but it is equally true that he is a citizen of the state. By taking a federal office he cannot avoid his duty

[40] 26 Cong. Rec., Part 9, Appendix, Part I, p. 4 ff. (53d Cong., 2d Sess.).

as a citizen; and his obligation to perform the duties of his office cannot absolve him from obedience to the law of the Commonwealth. . . .

"I have no hesitation in saying that any law of Congress impairing directly or indirectly this reserved right of the state is unconstitutional, and that the penalty of the state law would be imposed upon a postmaster offending against it, though he should plead his duty to obey such unconstitutional act of Congress."

Tucker's memorandum was sent to Postmaster General Holt, who cited Cushing's opinion (which Tucker had not seen), and ruled against the supremacy of the federal law. "The people of Virginia," said Holt, "may not only forbid the introduction and dissemination of such documents within their borders, but if brought there in the mails they may, by appropriate legal proceeding, have them destroyed. They have the same right to extinguish firebrands thus impiously hurled into the midst of their houses and altars that a man has to pluck the burning fuse from a bombshell which is about to explode at his feet."

It would seem, however, that such reasoning, while careful and persuasive, is erroneous. At the time these opinions were rendered, the absolute supremacy of federal law, when constitutionally enacted, was not accepted without question. It is true that, prior to this, provision had been made for the removal, before trial, of a prosecution arising under the revenue laws of the United States, and also that federal judges should have power to grant writs of *habeas corpus* in all cases of a prisoner or prisoners in jail or confinement "where he or they shall be committed or confined on, or by any authority or law, for any act done, or omitted to be done in pursuance of a law of the United States, or any order, process or decree of any judge or court thereof."[41]

To be sure, this was only a means of checking state action, but from the doctrine of federal supremacy it logically follows that it is not within the power of a state to punish

[41] Act of March 2, 1833 (4 Stat. L. 632).

acts done under authority of federal law. At the time the question of incendiary publications was acute, the Supreme Court had not decided the line of cases upholding the right of removal to federal courts and sanctioning the release of officers for acts done in pursuance of federal authority. These cases declared it to be "an incontrovertible principle that the government of the United States may, by means of physical force exercised through its agents, execute on every foot of American soil, the powers and functions that belong to it. This necessarily involves the power to command obedience to its laws, and hence the power to keep the peace to that extent. This power to enforce its laws and to execute its functions does not derogate from the power of the states to execute its laws at the same time and in the same places. The one does not exclude the other, except where both cannot be executed at the same time. In that case the words of the Constitution itself show which is to yield. 'This Constitution, and all laws which shall be made in pursuance thereof . . . shall be the supreme law of the land.'"[42]

And on the basis of this principle, there is no reason to hold that the postal employees could not be punished for distributing the incendiary matter when it was their federal duty so to do. To be sure, as urged by Cushing and Tucker, the United States guarantees each state a republican form of government and protects it against domestic violence, but this does not mean that a law which is passed by Congress to apply uniformly to the whole country, and which may, on account of peculiar local conditions, aid insurrectionary movements in certain of the states, is thereby unconstitutional. The resort of the states is not to the courts, but to Congress for the repeal of the harmful measure. Furthermore, the guarantee does not obligate the United States to insure a state against the occurrence of any violence, but

[42] Ex parte Siebold, 100 U. S. 371 (1879). See also Tennessee v. Davis, 100 U. S. 257 (1879), and 1 Willoughby on the Constitution, 124.

simply to protect it when the violence is attempted. Since, therefore, the federal laws made criminal the detention of any mail matter, with only such exceptions as Congress might introduce, there was no way in which the states might enforce their laws against incendiary literature, unless they could exclude it absolutely from their borders.

As to this power, there are no judicial precedents, but the carriage of the mails being under federal auspices and Congress having a property right in them, the authority of the states to exclude, if it exists at all, is certainly narrower than that in regard to interstate commerce. As to this, the states may exclude from their borders only such articles as are intrinsically unfit for commerce and unmerchantable. The Supreme Court enumerated, as examples, "rags or other substances infected with the germs of yellow fever, or the virus of small pox, or cattle, or meat or other provisions that are diseased or decayed." These articles "may be rightly outlawed as intrinsically and directly the immediate sources and causes of destruction to human health and life."[43] Publications calculated to incite the slaves to rebellion would not fall within this classification. The conclusion, then, must be that in disseminating the incendiary literature, the postal agents acted properly, and that the state laws were inoperative as applied to them. But if the states have a restricted power of exclusion, such as that defined in the Bowman case, it is, in effect, a nullity, since circumstances can hardly be imagined under which its exercise might take place, without delaying the mails, or violating federal statutes which attach penalties for opening the mail and interfering with it while *in transitu.*

There remains the further question whether a state is competent to forbid its citizens to receive certain mail matter, and here also the interstate commerce analogy affords an answer. By a long line of decisions, principally in regard to intoxicating liquors, it has been established

[43] Bowman v. Chicago & Northwestern R. Co., 125 U. S. 465 (1888).

that a state may not interfere with a commodity until it has reached the consignee, who has a right to receive shipments from without the state.[44] If the state forbids possession, no matter how acquired, then the question of receiving becomes academic, since it would be impossible to separate the two acts. So also, if Congress has excluded a commodity from interstate commerce, then the consignee's right to receive this commodity has been taken away, and the state has plenary power.[45] The same reasoning applies to the receiving of mail matter: the state would be competent to punish only if Congress has forbidden the use of the mails, as is the case, for example, with lottery tickets and obscene literature. But in any event, a law directed against receiving certain mail matter could just as well forbid possession, and as the state has power in the latter case, the distinction is without importance except in so far as the possession is more difficult to detect than the receipt. Certain it is, however, that, as was attempted by the incendiary literature legislation, the state may not punish a man for taking from the mails what the federal government permits to be sent.

This conclusion is applicable to the validity of legislation forbidding the advertisement of intoxicating liquors. The state may not keep out, or prevent the receipt of, such advertisements or journals containing them, when sent through the mails or interstate commerce; it may forbid the sale of such journals if not in their "original packages,"[46] and if it attempts to penalize the possession of such advertisements, there is no constitutional question so far as the mails are concerned.

The use of the mails may constitute a crime against the state, but the Circuit Court of Appeals for the Fourth Cir-

[44] See, *inter alia,* Leisy v. Hardin, 135 U. S. 100 (1890), and Rhodes v. Iowa, 170 U. S. 412 (1897).

[45] This is the theory of the Webb-Kenyon Act. See my papers, "The Power of the States over Commodities Excluded by Congress from Interstate Commerce," 24 Yale Law Journal, 567 (May, 1915), and "State Legislation under the Webb-Kenyon Act." 28 Harvard Law Review, 225 (January, 1915).

[46] See the reasoning in State v. Delaye, 68 So. 993 (Ala., 1915).

cuit has gone much farther than previous decisions and in a recent case declared: "It makes no difference that the United States Mail was used for the solicitation [of orders for intoxicating liquors]. The federal government does not protect those who use its mails to thwart the police regulations of a state made for the conservation of the welfare of its citizens. The use of the mail is a mere incident in carrying out the illegal act, and affords no more protection in a case like this than a like use of the mails to promote a criminal conspiracy, or to perpetrate a murder by poison, or to solicit contributions of office holders in violation of the civil service law, or to obtain goods under false pretenses."[47]

In Adams v. The People[48]—the case probably meant but not cited by the last clause of the quotation—there was an indictment for obtaining money under false pretenses, although the defendant was a resident of Ohio and had never been in New York. So also, in cases referred to by the Circuit Court of Appeals, the solicitation through the mails of orders for intoxicating liquors has been punished where the matter was mailed and received within the limits of the state and there was no interstate commerce involved.[49] But the Supreme Court decisions cited by the Circuit Court of Appeals simply hold that Congress may make the use of the mails a crime when in furtherance of a purpose to violate federal laws and are obviously not precedents for sustaining the West Virginia legislation.[50]

Now, the *sine qua non* of forbidding solicitation by means of the postoffice is that the sale of the intoxicating liquor is itself a crime; otherwise the state could have an unrestrained power to prescribe the purposes for which the mails might be used. The Circuit Court of Appeals evidently reasoned on this basis and considered as constitutional the

[47] West Virginia v. Adams Express Co., 219 Fed. Rep. 794 (1915).

[48] 1 N. Y. 173 (1848).

[49] Hayner v. State, 83 Ohio St. 178 (1910). See also Zinn v. State, 83 Ark. 273, 114 S. W. 227 (1908).

[50] U. S. v. Thayer, 209 U. S. 39 (1908), and In re Palliser, 136 U. S. 257 (1890).

section of the state law which provides that "in case of a sale in which a shipment or delivery of such liquors is made by a common or other carrier, the sale thereof shall be deemed to be made in the county wherein the delivery thereof is made by such carrier to the consignee, his agent, or employee." The Court held that such a regulation was sanctioned by the Webb-Kenyon Act,[51] although admittedly invalid if not thus justified. This presents a question that is beyond the purview of the present study, but it is obvious that if the sales could be made, then the solicitation could not be made a crime; and it may be added, parenthetically, that the Court probably erred in holding that the sales were forbidden.

The case nearest in point—Rose Co. v. State[52]—is not cited by the Circuit Court's opinion. The defendant corporation in Tennessee mailed circulars advertising liquors to residents of Barton County, Ga. The Georgia law forbade solicitations where it was unlawful to sell, but the Supreme Court of Georgia held that shipments could be made from without the state under the protection of the commerce clause, and it could not, therefore, be a crime to use a federal agency in furtherance of a purpose that was sanctioned by the Federal Constitution.

It may be said, then, that the use of the mails may be penalized only when in furtherance of a purpose that is unlawful; nor can it be argued—as was done with considerable force by the late James C. Carter against the exclusion of lottery tickets from the mails[53]—that the state may punish only when the purposes are *mala in se* and not when merely *mala prohibita*. If the state has the power, it may define "unlawful," but punishment cannot take place if the act

[51] 37 Stat. L. 699. For a further discussion of this point see my paper, "Unlawful Possession of Intoxicating Liquors and the Webb-Kenyon Act," 16 Columbia Law Review, 1 (1916).

[52] 133 Ga. 353, 65 S. E. 770, 36 L. R. A. (n. s.) 443 (1909), and note, which says that the case is one *primae impressionis*. It should be said that the decision in the Court of Appeals was *contra*. See 4 Ga. App. 588, 62 S. E. 117 (1908).

[53] In re Rapier, 143 U. S. 110 (1892).

sought to be effected by the use of the mails is permitted by state law, or if the inhibition is invalid, as is, it would seem, the case with the West Virginia legislation. Finally, it is difficult to see how the state may forbid anything but direct solicitation. A magazine or newspaper proprietor who publishes the advertisements does not use the mails for the purpose of consummating a crime, and the advertiser does not use the mails at all. The solicitation, therefore, must be direct.[54]

[54] To make the record complete it should be added that the federal courts have exclusive jurisdiction of all offenses embraced by statute, committed in a postoffice owned by the United States or jurisdiction over which has been ceded by the state. Battle v. U. S., 209 U. S. 36 (1908). But the fact that a train is engaged exclusively in carrying the United States mail does not preclude the jurisdiction of a state court of a prosecution for the murder of an engineer, committed by derailing the train. Crossley v. California, 168 U. S. 640 (1898).

CHAPTER VI

The Extension of Federal Control over Postroads

Federal Ownership of Railroads.—In an address at Indianapolis on May 30, 1907, President Roosevelt discussing the necessity for further congressional regulation of railway companies, declared that, "in so far as the common carriers also transport the mails, it is, in my opinion, probable that whether their business is or is not interstate, it is to the same extent subject to federal control, under that clause of the Constitution granting to the national government power to establish postroads, and therefore by necessary implication power to take all action necessary in order to keep them at the highest point of efficiency."[1]

The placing of such a construction upon the postroads clause aroused a storm of criticism, but, in the main, President Roosevelt was correct in his assertion of congressional authority. Municipal streets used by mail carriers or wagons are postroads and federal control exists to the extent of insuring safe passage of the mail and prohibiting private competition; by the rural free delivery system, moreover, state wagon roads are under federal authority to the same extent. That much has been made evident by the preceding discussion.

As to common carriers between the states, congressional regulation has been very largely based upon the commerce clause of the Federal Constitution, and the transportation

[1] The Roosevelt Policy, vol. ii, p. 486. In his Provincetown address (August 20, 1907) President Roosevelt returned to the same theme, saying: "I believe, furthermore, that the need for action is most pressing as regards those corporations which, because they are common carriers, exercise a quasi-public function; and which can be completely controlled, in all respects, by the federal government by the exercise of the power conferred under the interstate commerce clause, and, if necessary, under the post-road clause of the Constitution." Ibid., p. 564.

of the mails has been a secondary, not primary, ground to justify the authority exerted. This commercial power does not extend to intrastate undertakings, but if these were concerned with furnishing postal facilities they could be brought under federal control. This doctrine, however, should be carefully qualified so as not to assert a right in Congress to assume general supervision, for example, of municipal traction companies, an incidental function of which is to carry the mails. The control could be exerted only so far as was reasonably necessary to insure the safe, speedy, and unobstructed transportation of government property.

This control, as the Debs[2] case made clear, is, in the case of interstate carriers at least, and by parity of reasoning in the case of intrastate undertakings also, not confined to mere legislative rules, enforceable in the courts, but the executive power may remove obstructions to the carriage of the mails. The national government is charged "with the duty of keeping those highways of interstate commerce free from obstruction, for it has always been recognized as one of the powers and duties of a government to remove obstructions from the highways under its control." On this power rests, in large part, at least, the act of October 1, 1888,[3] providing for arbitration between railroad companies and their employees and subsequent acts for the same purpose. The full power has not yet been exerted; it extends to the compulsory settlement of such disputes (subject to the limitations of the Thirteenth Amendment),[4] and to the enforcement by federal authority of such regulations as may be necessary to remove obstructions and insure the carriage of the mails without delay, even in the case of streets within a town and with reference to municipal traction companies.

It is no longer open to doubt that the federal government, under its right of eminent domain, upon the payment of adequate compensation judicially determined, may compel service from railroads by which existing terms for the car-

[2] 158 U. S. 564 (1895).
[3] 25 Stat. L. 501.
[4] See 2 Willoughby on the Constitution, 855.

riage of the mails may have been deemed unsatisfactory. This may be done either by assuming the temporary management of the roads for such a purpose, or by enforcing criminal provisions against obstructing or delaying the mails. While such a power has not been exercised, it certainly exists.[5]

But the Senate Committee which in 1874 declared that the government could thus compel the transportation of the mails, went still further and maintained that Congress could "take absolutely, on paying just compensation therefor, without the consent either of the owner or of the state within which such road may be, any railroad, its rolling stock and equipments, within the United States for the public use and transportation over the same of the United States mails,"—an advanced position for this period when Congress had as yet attempted slight regulation of the railroads.

It should require but little argument, I think, to show that if Congress decides to nationalize the railways of the country it may constitutionally do so under its power to establish postroads. Federal charters to railroads and bridge companies have been pitched upon the postal, commercial, and war powers; they have granted rights of way through the states, immunity from taxation, powers of eminent domain, and the right of resort to the federal courts on the ground of federal citizenship. Congress has, moreover, the right of eminent domain even for patriotic purposes,—to preserve the Gettysburg battlefield,—a much more remote public purpose than that of establishing postal facilities under the specific authorization in the Constitution.[6]

In Osborn v. The Bank of the United States,[7] it was urged upon the Supreme Court that the bank was not an instrument of the government and a distinction was drawn between it and an agency for which provision was made in

[5] 43d Cong., 1st Sess., Senate Rept. No. 478.

[6] California v. Pacific Railroad Companies, 127 U. S. 1 (1887); U. S. v. Gettysburg Electric Co., 160 U. S. 668 (1896).

[7] 9 Wheat. 738 (1824).

the Constitution. "The postoffice is established by the general government," said counsel. "It is a public institution. The persons who perform its duties are public officers. No individual has or can acquire any property in it. For all services performed a compensation is paid out of the national treasury; and all money received upon account of its operations is public property." The business "is of a public character and the charge of it expressly conferred upon Congress by the Constitution."[8] This distinction between the public nature of postal facilities and the private character of much of the business done by the bank was urged to show that the latter was subject to taxation by the state.

To this argument Chief Justice Marshall replied that if the premises were true, the conclusion would be inevitable. But there was a political connection between the bank and the government and "Congress was of the opinion that these faculties [of doing private business] were necessary to enable the bank to perform the services which are exacted from it, and for which it was created. . . . That the exercise of these faculties greatly facilitates the fiscal operations of the government is too obvious for controversy: and who will venture to affirm that the suppression of them would not materially affect these operations, and essentially impair, if not totally destroy, the utility of the machine to the government?" If the private business engaged in has the result of making the corporation "a more fit instrument for the purposes of the government than it otherwise would be," then "the capacity to carry on this trade is a faculty indispensable to the character and objects of the institution."

There can be no question of the right of the federal government itself to construct highways for the transportation of the mail and to charge tolls for their use; nor can there be any doubt of its power to own and operate carriers, and incidentally to engage in business of a private nature if this increases the efficiency of the governmental agency.

---

[8] 9 Wheat. 785 (1824).

Even the fact that these private undertakings, disassociated from the carriage of the mails, would be by far the most important, would make no difference, according to the rule as announced by Chief Justice Marshall. On this theory, moreover, can be justified the assumption by the federal government of the functions of a bank and common carrier, through the postal savings and money order systems, and the parcel post, even though these activities can also be supported as proper elements of a postal power as it is interpreted in other countries.

If, therefore, the federal government is competent to establish postal facilities and use them for ancillary yet helpful purposes, there is no reason why it may not exercise its power of eminent domain and take possession of any or all agencies now used in the transportation of the mails, upon the payment of just compensation; own and operate these agencies, use them to carry the mails, and to perform all other functions which would "greatly facilitate the fiscal operations of the government." In this would, of course, be included the smaller power of creating a corporation, perhaps owned in part by the government, to take over and operate the railroads of the country for the same purposes. The connection between such a corporation and the government would be political and public as Marshall pointed out, but it would be created to carry out a power specifically mentioned in the Constitution, and its public nature would therefore be much more apparent. There is thus an error of understatement when it is urged that "no valid distinction can be drawn between the vital necessity of the right to trade in money to a fiscal instrumentality of the government, and the right to trade in transportation to a transportation instrumentality of the government."[9]

It is an arguable proposition that such a purpose could be accomplished under the commercial power which is simply that of "regulation." By many the opinion is held that this of itself is sufficient to give Congress the right to compel

[9] Farrar, The Post Road Power (Hearings before Committee on Interstate Commerce, United States Senate, 62d Congress, p. 1498 ff).

industrial corporations doing an interstate business to secure federal charters. The constitutionality of a law to compel interstate railroads to incorporate under the commerce clause is even less doubtful, and the Supreme Court has upheld the exercise of the commercial power in condemning the property of a state corporation organized to improve navigation, just compensation including the value of the franchise which was destroyed.[10] Federal incorporation, then, may be required on the ground that it is necessary for the efficient regulation of the carriers. On the other hand, the postal clause gives Congress the right to establish instrumentalities for the transportation of the mails, and the assumption of control or ownership under this grant of power is more surely within the rule as laid down by Marshall in Osborn v. The Bank of the United States.

In 1792 the proposal was made in Congress that the proprietors of mail stages be permitted to carry passengers, but the motion was lost, on the ground that under the postal clause Congress did not provide the necessary authority.[11] It is true, also, that the framers of the Constitution did not, because they could not, contemplate the taking over by Congress of the railways of the country. And, as the preceding discussion has attempted to show, during the early days of legislative activity under the postroads clause, the consent of the states was required for construction within their borders, and they acceded in one form or another to several of the acts granting federal charters.[12] But, as the Supreme Court of the United States has said in language already quoted, the powers of Congress "are not confined to the instrumentalities of commerce or of the postal service known or in use when the Constitution was adopted, but they keep pace with the progress of the country." This, coupled with the right of eminent domain, is, it is submitted, sufficient to enable the national government, either

---

[10] Monongahela Navigation Co. v. U. S., 148 U. S. 312 (1893).

[11] Annals of 2d Congress, pp. 303–309.

[12] See Prentice, Federal Power over Corporations and Carriers, p. 152.

directly or through a federally chartered corporation, to take over and operate the railroads of the country for the carriage of the mails, with the power of engaging in the transportation of freight or passengers, to the extent that Congress may desire.[13]

Postal Telegraphs and Telephones.—The case last cited is ample authority for Congress to take over and operate the telegraph and telephone systems of the country, for the Supreme Court made its pronouncement in upholding the act of July 24, 1866,[14] "to aid in the construction of telegraph lines, and to secure to the government the use of the same for postal, military and other purposes." The act, among other things, gave companies complying with its terms the right to erect their poles and string their wires along any military or post road, and the Supreme Court declared void a state statute which attempted to give exclusive rights to a local company.

By the third section of the congressional act, it was provided that "the United States may, at any time after the expiration of five years from the date of the passage of this act, for postal, military or other purposes, purchase all the telegraph lines, property and effects of any or all of said companies at an appraised value, to be ascertained by five competent, disinterested persons, two of whom shall be selected by the postmaster general of the United States, two by the company interested, and one by the four so previously selected." The United States therefore reserved to itself the power which it would otherwise have had,—that of eminent domain in respect to telegraph facilities. In his report for 1913, the postmaster general said:

"A study of the constitutional purposes of the postal establishment leads to the conviction that the Post Office De-

---

[13] Pensacola Telegraph Co. v. Western Union Telegraph Co., 96 U. S. 1 (1878). Congress may authorize the secretary of war to lease upon terms agreed upon any excess of water power which results from the conservation of the flow of a river, and the works which the government may construct. U. S. v. Chandler-Dunbar Water Power Co., 229 U. S. 53 (1913).

[14] 37 Stat. L. 560.

partment should have control over all means of the communication of intelligence. The first telegraph line in this country was maintained and operated as a part of the postal service, and it is to be regretted that Congress saw fit to relinquish this facility to private enterprise. The monopolistic nature of the telegraph business makes it of vital importance to the people that it be conducted by unselfish interests, and this can be accomplished only through government ownership." If Congress decides to take over these facilities, its action will be clearly within the postal power.[15]

[15] For an account of proposals in Congress to take this action, a history of its recommendation by successive postmasters general, and much valuable statistical information concerning the operation of the American privately owned, and the foreign publicly owned, telegraph and telephone systems, see "Government Ownership of Electrical Means of Communication," 63d Congress, 2d Sess., Senate Doc. No. 399.

CHAPTER VII

THE EXTENSION OF FEDERAL CONTROL THROUGH EXCLUSION FROM THE MAILS

It has already been indicated that, while the postal power of Congress is plenary, extending to the classification and exclusion of articles presented for transmission through the mails, it is not without limits; that its exercise is restricted by provisions found in the Constitution itself,—the guarantees of a free press and immunity from unreasonable searches and seizures. There is, moreover, a further important limitation in that an arbitrary refusal of postal facilities would seem to be a denial of due process of law.

The Supreme Court of the United States has not yet been called upon to set any limit to congressional action under this clause; it has thus far upheld every law restricting the use of the postoffice. But it should be remembered in the discussion which follows that all existing exclusions from the mails can be justified as partaking of the nature of police regulations; the prohibited articles are either inherently injurious, inimical to the health, safety and well being of recipients, or the use of the mails is denied because it would be in furtherance of a design that is condemned by moral considerations or is against public policy.

That this *Index Expurgatorius* will be extended may be taken for granted. It is in the nature of police regulations that they expand more inclusively and rigorously. For example, in 1912 Congress excluded from the mails moving picture films of prize fights.[1] At the third session of the Sixty-third Congress, moreover, bills were introduced and urged to deny absolutely the use of the mails to any person who, in the opinion of the postmaster general, "is engaged

[1] 37 Stat. L. 240.

or represents himself as engaged in the business of publishing" any books or pamphlets of an indecent, immoral, scurrilous or libelous character. No letter, packet, parcel, newspaper, book or other thing, said one bill, "sought to be sent through the postoffice by or on behalf or to or on behalf of such person shall be deemed mailable matter, and the postmaster general shall make the necessary rules and regulations to exclude such nonmailable matter from the mails."[2] The proposed legislation was aimed at certain publications devoted to the unrestrained, defamatory and often indecent criticism of particular religious denominations and their clergy.

The constitutionality of this legislation, however, is open to serious doubt. There can, of course, be no question as to the impairment of religious freedom, for, while this requires freedom of attack, it cannot "justify the violation of public order and common decency"; or, as put by another authority, "the prohibition does not prevent Congress from penalizing the commission of acts, which, although justified by the tenets of a religious sect, are socially or politically disturbing, or are generally reprobated by the moral sense of civilized communities."[3] Nor is the objection that the freedom of the press would be impaired, since, admitting that a denial of postal facilities would be an impairment of the liberty of publication, the federal guarantee does not include the right to publish scurrilous or libelous utterances on matters of private concern; or, to take Hamilton's test, there is no publication of truth, with good motives and for justifiable ends.[4]

If the proposed legislation simply made such matter nonmailable and penalized any attempt to use the postoffice for its carriage, it would probably be free from objection. But under the bill quoted above, if it was established that a

---

[2] See Exclusion of Certain Publications from the Mails, p. 3 ff. (Hearing before the Committee on the Postoffice and Postroads, House of Representatives, 63d Cong., 3d Sess.).

[3] Freund, Police Power, p. 509; 2 Willoughby on the Constitution, 841.

[4] Schofield, Freedom of the Press in the United States, p. 90.

person made a practice of sending such matter through the mails, the postmaster general would have the absolute authority arbitrarily to deny him facilities for *all* his mail matter, much of which would be admittedly innocuous; and whether, if the objectionable practices were suspended, the person would again be permitted to make use of the governmental agency, would depend on the discretion of the postmaster general. This official's authority would, in effect, be to punish for acts not made criminal by Congress. Such legislation would for this reason seem unconstitutional as well as ill-considered.

But this exclusion is in a class by itself. It is an attempt to reach effectively an evil over which there is admittedly some federal control, for Congress may prevent the transmission of scurrilous papers. The objection is to the method of exercise rather than to the existence of the power. Of a different character is the strongly urged proposal that congressional control of the mails may be used as a valid means to compel the performance or non-performance of certain acts by persons, over whom there exists no direct federal authority. In other words, it is contended that Congress has a plenary and arbitrary power to determine who shall use the mails and what articles shall be carried, and therefore may impose any antecedent conditions, no matter how onerous or remote, upon the enjoyment of postal facilities. With the ever increasing frequency and importance of problems demanding a solution by the federal government in the absence of effective, and in some cases even attempted, settlement by the states, Congress is under the necessity of casting about for indirect methods of exerting control, since direct action would be unconstitutional. The use for this purpose of the taxing and commercial powers has in some instances been made, and in others is very strongly urged. It is also argued that Congress may refuse corporations, to whose size, organization, or activities, it objects, the right to sue in federal courts and that national banks may be ordered not to receive their deposits. In asking, therefore, whether it is constitutional for Congress to exert such indirect control under the cloak of regulating the mails, we will merely consider one phase of the larger subject of indirect government.

Such an exercise of power over the mails has been advocated to secure corporate publicity. "Congress," says one who is in favor of such extension of federal control, "by regulating the use of the mails and channels of interstate commerce, may compel every corporation engaged in any business, *whether interstate or not,* to give publicity to its corporate affairs, by legislation denying the use of the mails and the instruments of interstate commerce for the transmission of any matter concerning the affairs or business of any corporation that fails to make and file reports of the fullest nature concerning its organization and business, such, for example, as are already exacted from interstate carriers under the Interstate Commerce Act. Such legislation would be valid and enforceable."[5]

It has been suggested in Congress[6] that an effective punitive method of dealing with monopolistic corporations would be to deny them postal facilities.[7] If such corporations were violating the Sherman Act or were otherwise outlawed by valid legislation, Congress would have the right to deny them the use of the mails, since it would be absurd for the general government to aid, through its instrumentalities, persons or corporations violating laws which it had passed. An illustrative case is afforded by the provision of the Panama Canal Act of August 24, 1912, which says that no

[5] Pam, "Powers of Regulation Vested in Congress," 24 Harvard Law Review, 77 (December, 1910).

[6] As stated by Senator Newlands: "Congress can prohibit the use of the mails by any organization which it considers unlawful or injurious to the public welfare. It can, therefore, declare that any combination organized for the purpose of monopolizing the manufacture, production or sale of any article of commerce, or for the purpose of preventing competition is illegal, and can forbid and prohibit the use of the mails of the United States in aid of such business." 33 Cong. Rec. (App.), p. 675. See also Remarks of Lanham, 33 Cong. Rec., p. 6324.

[7] This was rejected by a House Committee on the ground that it was inadequate. See 56th Cong., 1st Sess., House Rept. No. 1501.

vessel owned by any company doing business in violation of any of the acts of Congress relating to interstate commerce "shall be permitted to enter or pass through said canal."[8]

But it is a different proposition to urge that Congress may deny the use of the mails in order to compel corporate publicity, when, if the legislation directly commanded compliance, it would be clearly *ultra vires*. Thus, the Pujo Money Trust Committee proposed "that Congress prohibit the transmission by the mails or by telegraph or telephone from one state to another of orders to buy or sell or quotations or other information concerning transactions on any stock exchange, unless [among other conditions] such exchange shall (1) be a body corporate of the state or territory in which it is located."[9] This proposal was based upon the conclusion of a majority of the committee that "Congress has power to prevent the use of the mails to disseminate

[8] 37 Stat. L. 560 (sec. 11). See also Mr. Adamson's bill, H. R. 9576, 63d Cong., 2d Sess. (December 1, 1913).

[9] Majority Report of the Committee Appointed to Investigate the Concentration of Control of Money and Credit (February 28, 1913), p. 162. A bill embodying these recommendations is given on p. 170. It denies the use of the mails to any stock exchange, "unless such exchange has been incorporated under the laws of the state or territory at which its business is conducted, or unless the charter and by-laws of such exchange or the law under which it is organized shall contain regulations and prohibitions satisfactory to the Postmaster General safeguarding the transactions of such exchange, the character of the securities dealt in thereon, the genuineness of the quotations thereof, and all other information concerning such transactions that is to be carried through the mails, and by telegraph and telephone beyond the limits of the state of the organization of such exchange against fraud and deceit in the following particulars": These require publicity as to the assets and stock issues of a corporation before its securities may be listed; an annual report by the corporation whose securities are listed, to the secretary of the exchange and the postmaster general, giving a detailed statement of receipts, expenses, net earnings, salaries and commissions paid to officers or directors, etc.; prohibition of arbitrary action by a stock exchange in striking securities from its list, of artificial manipulation of securities, of hypothecation of securities purchased on a margin, of "short-selling," etc. The bill also contains many requirements as to publicity. For a discussion of the economic features of the Pujo Committee's proposals, see Regulation of the Stock Exchange, p. 585 ff. (Hearings before the Committee on Banking and Currency, United States Senate, 63d Cong., 2d Sess.).

quotations or other information concerning transactions on stock exchanges whose facilities are used for purposes of gambling and price manipulation, and that exercising its wide choice of means to that end, it may prohibit the transmission through the mails of any information relating to transactions on exchanges refusing submission to regulations reasonably adapted to preventing the objectionable practices."[10]

The question arises whether such an exclusion would not violate the freedom of the press, since newspapers and other publications could not use the mails if they contained any information, however harmless and valuable, concerning any transactions (to which Congress might have no objection) of the exchange which has refused to accept regulations which the general government had no power directly to impose. Newspapers would be unable to circulate truth on matters of public concern if the published information as to stock quotations, although harmless in its nature, concerned an institution whose practices Congress was indirectly attempting to check. If the law were carefully confined to the prohibition of the circulation of publications which contained matter relating to gambling transactions, there would be no abridgment of the guarantee of the First Amendment. The exclusion would be similar to that of lottery advertisements, or matter designed to aid in defrauding recipients. But as proposed by the Pujo Committee, the law would, at least in part, if not as a whole, operate as an abridgment of the freedom of the press.

Apart from this consideration, however, the theory of the law, differently stated, is that Congress, under its power to exclude from the mails gambling contracts and matter designed to defraud recipients, may go farther and exclude harmless matter because this seems a necessary and adequate means of compelling the exchanges to take out state charters, a concession thought by Congress to be desirable

[10] Majority Report, p. 122.

in order to prevent the gambling and other harmful practices, over which there is no direct national control.

Still other proposals would extend federal authority in a similar manner. It is urged, for example, that Congress prohibit the use of the mails by fire insurance companies which at present are, by means of the postoffice, able to do business in states where they could not, if they used local agents.[11] And to give a third example, it was argued that an efficient means of prohibiting trading in cotton futures would be to deny the use of the mails for the furtherance of such transactions.[12] The extent to which the Supreme Court has thus far recognized in Congress authority of this character, is only to sanction the refusal to lend federal aid, by furnishing postal facilities to the furtherance or consummation of gambling and fraudulent schemes.

One measure of a character somewhat analogous to those proposals which we have been considering, has, however, already been sustained by the Supreme Court of the United States. I refer to the recent so-called "Newspaper Publicity Law" which requires publications entered as second-class matter (with a few exceptions) to furnish the postoffice department with, and publish, a sworn statement giving the names and addresses of the owners, editors, and business managers, and, in the case of daily newspapers, circulation figures. It is provided that "any such publication shall be denied the privileges of the mail if it shall fail to comply with the provisions of this paragraph within ten days after notice by registered letter of such failure."[13]

---

[11] See S. 5664, 63d Cong., 2d Sess. (May 26, 1914).

[12] See Regulation of Cotton Exchanges, p. 310 ff. (Hearings before the Committee on Agriculture, House of Representatives (April, 1914)). See also 63d Cong., 2d Sess., House Rept. 765. It should be pointed out that the "trading in futures" that it was desired to prohibit was in the nature of gambling contracts and had come under the ban of local laws.

[13] 37 Stat. L. 553. A separate and concluding paragraph provides: "That all editorial or other reading matter published in any such newspaper, magazine or periodical, for the publication of which money or other valuable consideration is paid, accepted, or promised, shall be plainly marked 'advertisement.' Any editor or publisher printing editorial or other reading matter for which com-

As claimed in the defendants' brief, when the law went before the Supreme Court, Congress had, in effect, attempted "to regulate journalism." Relying upon its power over the postoffice, Congress had threatened those publications which enjoy second-class rates with a denial of this privilege should they refuse to comply with the conditions; and it was, moreover, made a crime to continue to use the mails and violate the stipulation that all reading matter for the publication of which a valuable consideration is received, "shall be plainly marked 'advertisement.'" Such regulations, without any reference to the use of the mails, would be obviously outside the constitutional power of Congress.

By a narrow, but nevertheless a convincing line of reasoning, the Supreme Court, through Chief Justice White, was able to justify the law without being put to the necessity of making any definite declaration as to the limits to which Congress may go in its exercise of what, lacking a better phrase, we may call "indirect regulation under the postal power."

The Court's opinion shows that in the classification of mail matter there has been no attempt at uniformity and that periodical publications have enjoyed special favors by reason of legislative adherence to what has been described as the "historic policy of encouraging by low postal rates the dissemination of current intelligence."[14] It is shown that as a condition precedent to being "entered as second class mail matter" and enjoying the low rates which are maintained at a loss, the government demands an answer to a score of questions concerning ownership, editorial

---

pensation is paid, accepted, or promised, without so marking the same, shall, upon conviction in any court having jurisdiction, be fined not less than fifty dollars ($50) nor more than five hundred dollars ($500)."

[14] Report of the Commission on Second-Class Mail Matter, p. 143. In his message of February 22, 1912, transmitting this report to Congress, President Taft said: "The findings of the commission confirm the view that the cost of handling and transporting second-class mail matter is greatly in excess of the postage paid, and that an increase in the rate is not only justified by the facts, but is desirable."

direction, advertising discrimination, specimen copies, and circulation. To the Third Assistant Postmaster General is given the authority of accepting or rejecting applications of entry at the second-class rate.[15] The Supreme Court simply considered the law as laying down new conditions, compliance with which will continue the right "to enjoy great privileges and advantages at the public expense." In its opinion the Court says:

"As the right to consider the character of the publication as an advertising medium was previously deemed to be incidental to the exercise of the power to classify for the purpose of the second class mail, it is impossible in reason to perceive why the new condition as to marking matter, which is paid for as an advertisement, is not equally incidental to the right to classify.

"And the additional exactions as to disclosure of stockholders, principals, creditors, etc., also are clearly incidental to the power to classify as are the requirements as to disclosure of ownership, editors, etc., which for so many years formed the basis of the right of admission to the classification. We say this because of the intimate relation which exists between ownership and debt. . . .

"Considered intrinsically, no completer statement of the relation which the newly exacted conditions bear to the great public purpose which induced Congress to continue in favor of the publishers of newspapers at vast public expense the low postal rate as well as other privileges accorded by the second class mail classification, can be made than was expressed in the report of the Senate Committee stating the intent of the legislation—that is, to secure to the public 'in the dissemination of knowledge of current events' by means of newspapers, the names, not only of the apparent, but of what might prove to be the real and substantial owners of the publications and to enable the public to know whether the matter which was published was

[15] Postal Laws and Regulations of 1913, p. 223.

what it purported to be, or was in substance a paid advertisement.

"We repeat that in considering this subject we are concerned not with any general regulation of what should be published in newspapers, nor with any condition excluding from the right to resort to the mails, but we are concerned solely and exclusively with the right on behalf of the publishers to continue to enjoy great privileges and advantages at the public expense, a right given them by Congress upon condition of compliance with regulations deemed by that body incidental and necessary to the complete fruition of the public policy lying at the foundation of the privileges accorded."[16]

This decision thus applies simply to the suspension of second class privileges and not to any general denial of the use of the mails. It is significant, moreover, that the Court expressly refused assent to the contention of the government, which as paraphrased in the opinion, was that the law merely "imposes conditions necessary to be complied with to enable publishers to participate in the great and exclusive privileges and advantages which arise from the right to use the second-class mail," but that even if "the provision be given the significance attributed to it by the publishers, it is valid as an exertion by Congress of its power to establish postoffices and post roads, a power which conveys an absolute right of legislative selection as to what shall be carried in the mails, and which, therefore, is not in anywise subject to judicial control even though in a given case it may be manifest that a particular exclusion is but arbitrary because resting on no discernible distinction nor coming within any discoverable principle of justice or public policy."

The Court, however, emphatically refused to accept this view, saying that "because there has developed no necessity of passing on the question, we do not wish even by the remotest implication to be regarded as assenting to the broad contentions concerning the existence of arbitrary

[16] Lewis Publishing Co. v. Morgan, 229 U. S. 288 (1913).

power through the classification of the mails, or by way of condition, embodied in the proposition of the government which we have previously stated."

The Supreme Court has, however, permitted Congress, in the exercise of its taxing power, and less noticeably in its control of interstate commerce, to accomplish ends which were not included in the enumerated delegations of the Constitution. Thus, the tax on state bank notes which made their issue unprofitable was upheld on the ground that "the judiciary cannot prescribe to the legislative department of the government limitations upon the exercise of its *acknowledged* powers. The power to tax may be exercised oppressively upon persons, but the responsibility of the legislature is not to the courts, but to the people by whom its members are elected."[17] Such a position in this case, however, was easily justified on the ground that Congress had the power to stop altogether the issue of the state bank notes if it thought that this course was necessary in order to provide an effective currency system, and the case thus loses much of its apparent importance.[18]

More illustrative, perhaps, of the plenary power of Congress with respect to the raising of a revenue, and impossible to justify on such a ground, is the decision upholding a tax upon oleomargarine so heavy that it can only be manufactured at a loss. Thus, unable directly to control manufacture, Congress has achieved the same end through the exercise of its taxing power. The Supreme Court said:

The argument "when reduced to its last analysis comes to this: that because a particular department of the government may exert its lawful powers with the object or motive of reaching an end not justified, therefore it becomes the duty of the judiciary to restrain the exercise of a lawful power whenever it seems to the judicial mind that such

---

[17] Veazie v. Fenno, 8 Wall. 533 (1869). Italics mine.

[18] In Edye v. Robertson, 112 U. S. 580 (1884) the Supreme Court said that the imposition "was upheld because a means properly adopted by Congress to protect the currency which it had created," and the tax was not, therefore, subject to the ordinary rules.

lawful power has been abused. But this reduces itself to the contention that under our constitutional system, the abuse by one department of the government of its lawful powers is to be corrected by the abuse of its powers by another department."[19]

Such reasoning is, it appears, final, although it goes farther than the Bank Note Case which declared that "there are indeed certain virtual limitations arising from the principles of the Constitution itself. It would undoubtedly be an abuse of the power [that of taxation] if so exercised as to impair the separate existence and independent self government of the states or if exercised for ends inconsistent with the limited grants of power in the Constitution."[20] However, although with more guarded language, the Court, even in the McCray case, intimated that a judicial veto might attach to measures which on their face bore evidence of not being tax laws at all, but were transparent in their purpose to control subjects not within the power of Congress. Such a law has not come before the Supreme Court.

Not so striking, but nevertheless important illustrations of this "nullification by indirection"[21] are to be found in the interstate commerce legislation of recent years. Congress has excluded lottery tickets from interstate commerce on account of their harmful effect on recipients;[22] it has

---

[19] McCray v. U. S., 197 U. S. 27 (1903).

[20] Veazie v. Fenno, above. The distinction has sometimes been drawn between *acknowledged* powers and *implied* powers of Congress. For example, the power to tax and to regulate interstate commerce is granted in the Constitution, while that to exclude from the mails is implied from the postal clause. From this it is argued that Congress may be limited in its indirect control under an *implied* power when the same objection would not apply to the exercise of an *acknowledged* power. (See the brief of James M. Beck in the newspaper publicity case, printed in Cong. Rec., December 11, 1912.) But this distinction has never been sanctioned by the Supreme Court of the United States.

It is proper, however, in this connection to point out the extraordinary nature of the taxing power, which is, in Marshall's phrase, the "power to destroy."

[21] The term is Mr. J. M. Beck's. See his brief in Lewis Publishing Co. v. Morgan, supra, and his article, "Nullification by Indirection," 23 Harvard Law Review, 441.

[22] Champion v. Ames, 188 U. S. 321 (1902).

assumed a control over the manufacture of food products by establishing standards of purity which must be met before the articles may begin an interstate journey.[23] The Mann White Slave Act extends federal control to immorality in the states, and in its decision upholding this law, the Supreme Court frankly admits that the means exerted "may have the quality of police regulations."[24] Proposals are now made to control manufacturing and trading companies, whether interstate or not, by compelling them to take out federal charters and modify their business practices (over which Congress has no direct control) in accordance with federal regulations before they will be permitted to enjoy the facilities of interstate commerce. It is most strongly urged that the national legislature has the power to improve labor conditions within the states, the most desired manifestation being a law putting articles made by children under specified ages in the same class with lottery tickets and impure foods.

Up to this time, however, legislation under the commerce clause has developed little necessity for passing upon the question whether these ultimate purposes may be considered by the courts, for the indirect control effected by the various acts is purely incidental in character. It is quite proper for Congress to build up an *Index Expurgatorius* just as it has done in the case of the mails, and to say that commerce shall not be "polluted" by the carriage of obscene literature, impure food, and made an agency to promote immorality. In every case, the power has been exerted on *things,* not on *persons,* and only once has there been even an apparent departure from this theory. Here the Supreme Court by a forced interpretation of the statute destroyed much of its force. I refer to the "commodities clause" of the Hepburn Bill which made it unlawful for any railroad to transport, except for its own use, any commodity other than timber which it had manufactured, mined, or pro-

[23] Hippolite Egg Co. v. U. S., 220 U. S. 45 (1911).
[24] Hoke v. U. S., 227 U. S. 308 (1913).

duced, or in which it had any interest. The Court interpreted this as meaning that the railroad was not forbidden to engage in mining, but that before transporting the product, it had to divorce itself from any interest by a *bona fide* sale. Such legislation, however, was "necessary and proper" in order to insure the enforcement of the regulations providing for equality of rates, publications of tariffs, etc. Any other interpretation would have required the Court to consider and decide several very "grave constitutional questions" as to the powers of Congress to regulate the production and ownership of commodities simply because they might become subjects of interstate commerce.[25]

But conceding the authority of Congress to regulate child labor indirectly, upon what theory is it based? In the words of a reluctant convert, "the lottery case is authority for the doctrine that interstate carriers may be prohibited from carrying, or shippers or manufacturers from sending from state to state and to foreign countries, commodities produced under conditions so objectionable as to be subject to control, as to their manufacture, by the states under an exercise of their police powers, or of a character designed or appropriate for a use which might similarly be forbidden by law."[26] Such legislation, however, would be directed against the articles produced under the objectionable conditions, and the manufacturers who employed child labor would not be prohibited from using the advantages of interstate commerce for other articles, not so produced.[27]

There is an obvious distinction between such legislation and that advocated by the money trust committee, a distinc-

25 U. S. ex rel. Atty. Gen. v. Delaware & H. Co., 213 U. S. 366 (1909).

26 Opinion of Prof. W. W. Willoughby, quoted by J. Y. Brinton, "The Constitutionality of a Federal Child Labor Law," 62 University of Pennsylvania Law Review, 501. See 2 Willoughby on the Constitution, 738.

27 A further argument in behalf of this legislation is that it would harmonize conflicting state laws which unduly operate in favor of certain manufacturers in their use of interstate commerce.

tion which is suggested, but not stressed, by the Solicitor General in the brief filed on behalf of the government in the newspaper publicity case: there must be no "regulation of the private business of citizens in a manner beyond any express or implied power of Congress" on the ground that such regulation "imposes as a penalty for disobedience a denial of an important federal privilege which Congress controls." Any legislation excluding from the mails must apply directly to the *things* mailed, not to the *persons* using the mails. This is a distinction which is evident in the decisions upholding the interstate commerce legislation, and which underlies the argument that Congress may exclude commodities manufactured in whole or in part by children. The law would operate directly on these commodities, not on account of their inherent character (which would probably not be different from that of other commodities manufactured by adult labor), but because of the objectionable conditions of production. And by a parity of reasoning, Congress could exclude from the mails matter relating to gambling transactions which might be forbidden under the police power of the state, although such matter, on its face, would be harmless. But it is an entirely different proposition absolutely to deny the use of the mails because certain persons have refused to comply with conditions, beyond the power of Congress directly to impose, which it thinks may result in regulating objectionable practices, although these may be entirely disassociated from the bulk of the matter which has been excluded.

The briefs of counsel on behalf of the Pujo Committee furnish no argument to change the opinion here expressed that the proposed legislation would be unconstitutional.[28] The validity of the bill is asserted on the ground of the

[28] Brief of Samuel Untermyer and Louis Marshall, Regulation of the Stock Exchange, p. 652 ff. This brief argues the matter at greater length than does the report of the Pujo Committee (p. 119 ff.), made the previous year and is in reply to the brief of counsel on behalf of the New York Stock Exchange (Regulation of the Stock Exchange, p. 570 ff.).

cases, already considered,[29] upholding the power of Congress to exclude lottery tickets and fraudulent matter. Chief importance, however, seems to be attached to a dictum of a District Court which says:

"If the use of the mails is a privilege which may be granted or withheld by Congress, Congress has the power to determine what shall be carried and what excluded . . . under the power to regulate the mails it has seen proper to declare that they shall not be used for any purposes which are detrimental to the morals of the people or against public policy, and by enacting that the sending of obscene matter through the mails shall not be permissible, it has determined such acts to be against public policy."[30] In this case the only matter before the court was the construction of the statute; there was no question as to the power of Congress, and the reasoning making public policy the test is clearly *obiter*. Counsel for the Pujo Committee, however, boldly argued as follows:

"It would therefore be within the competency of Congress, to prohibit absolutely the transmission through the mails of a circular or pamphlet or newspaper containing the quotations or information concerning transactions in securities on stock exchanges or otherwise, just as it has prohibited the transmission of circulars containing information with regard to lotteries. Such a prohibition may be absolute or conditional. Thus Congress might accompany a prohibition absolute in form with a proviso that its inhibition should not be applicable to" matter relating to securities "sold or offered for sale on a stock exchange duly incorporated, whose charter shall contain provisions similar to those set forth in the pending bill." Congress, the argu-

---

[29] Chapters II and IV. See also Burton v. U. S., 202 U. S. 344 (1909), where there is a *dictum* that the statute designed to prevent the postoffice from being used in aid of fraud "has its sanction in the power of the United States, by legislation, to designate what may be carried in the mails, and what must be excluded therefrom; such designation and exclusion to be, however, consistent with the rights of the people as reserved by the Constitution."

[30] U. S. v. Musgrave, 160 Fed. Rep. 700 (1908).

ment concludes, would simply be laying down a "rule as to what shall and what shall not be mailable matter, and in making this classification it is giving expression to what it conceives to be sound public policy, to the same extent and in the same way it does when it enacts any other kind of legislation that comes within the constitutional grant of legislative powers."[31]

But, it is submitted, Congress would be doing nothing of the sort. In the cases of the lottery tickets and obscene matter, the inhibition was on account of the inherent character of the matter mailed. If the test was one of public policy, as the very broad language of the District Court's opinion would seem to indicate, Congress simply declared it not sound public policy that the mails of the United States should be used in furtherance of transactions that were harmful. To be sure the Postmaster General is authorized to seize and detain all letters addressed to a person against whom a fraud order has issued, but this is justifiable on the ground that it is reasonably necessary in

[31] Regulation of the Stock Exchange, p. 657. The proposal in the Pujo Bill to deny unincorporated stock exchanges the use of the telephone or telegraph for the transmission of their quotations, raises the question whether Congress may exercise such indirect control under the guise of regulating interstate commerce. This question is discussed in the briefs (Regulation of the Stock Exchange, p. 570 ff. and p. 660 ff.), and is outside the purview of the present essay. From the brief review which I have attempted of the interstate commerce cases, however, it does not appear that they lend any support to the proposition contended for by the Pujo Committee. Generally speaking, the same principles are applicable, in relation to the power over interstate commerce as in relation to that over the mails as furnishing a means by which indirect control may be exerted. But it is proper to point out two possible differences: (1) an exclusion from interstate commerce is *prima facie* a "regulation" within the meaning of the grant in the Constitution; an exclusion from the mails, on the contrary, is not made "to establish postoffices," and it would seem, therefore, that the inhibition would have to be justified as "necessary and proper" to this end; (2) postal facilities are established and maintained by Congress for use, upon the same terms, by everyone standing in the same relation to the government, and it is therefore possible to argue that a denial of these facilities would be improper, when an equally arbitrary regulation of interstate commerce might not be. Neither of these differences, it may be added, is so clear as to be controlling; the first seems to me of probable importance, but the second, while it has been suggested, is of doubtful validity.

order to make effective the regulations against using the postoffice to defraud; but Congress has not yet made it a crime for anyone, some of whose mail matter may come within the inhibition, to deposit in, or take from, the mails, letters of a personal and harmless character. It is improper, then, to argue that in passing the Pujo Bill, Congress would act "to the same extent and in the same way" as it has done in the past. The authority of the fraud order decisions is simply that if Congress excludes matter relating to gambling transactions (as it probably has the right to do), correspondence deposited by or addressed to, the person suspected of unlawfully using the mails, may be seized and detained in order to make the gambling regulations effective. But the cases furnish no ground for the belief that Congress may penalize the use of the mails by these persons for the transmission of matter that is harmless. The brief of counsel for the Pujo Committee does not argue this point; nor does it take the natural, but nevertheless untenable, further position and maintain that Congress may make it a crime to deposit this harmless matter in order to detect violations of a law excluding information concerning gambling contracts.

On the contrary, counsel conceive the public policy of the proposed legislation to be the enforcement of the regulations set forth in the pending bill,—regulations that are not concerned with the character of the mail matter, but with persons using the mails. Not even by twisted interpretations can the adjudicated cases be made to support such reasoning. The "newspaper publicity law" which marks the extreme assertion of congressional authority, applies directly to the papers mailed. Only one *dictum,* of a *nisi prius* court,[32] lays down the test of public policy, and if, under its enumerated powers, Congress may legislate in fulfillment of this vague purpose, there would be a good deal of difficulty, I fancy, in showing that it would be subserved by the enforcement of the proposed regulations. And con-

---

[32] U. S. v. Musgrave, above.

ceding that Congress may control the postoffice on grounds of public policy, the fact that the ends to be attained are unconnected with the use of the mails, would prevent the legislative fiat from being final, and the enforcement of the Pujo Committee's recommendations would be so onerous and remote, that it would, I venture, not be permitted.[33] Reasoning such as that indulged in by the counsel, moreover, disregards the principle that runs through all the cases: the enforcement of postal regulations must be consistent with the rights reserved to the people. And the Pujo Bill attempts to regulate, not the mails, but stock exchanges.

The first Employers' Liability Case,[34] it is submitted, furnishes sufficient basis to uphold the correctness of the view that the proposed legislation is unconstitutional. In these cases it was held that the statute was not confined to a regulation of interstate commerce, but attempted to control *persons,* not only as to their engaging in interstate commerce, but in other respects, simply because some of their activities came under the authority of Congress. Furthermore, the Supreme Court has held that "there is no such connection between interstate commerce and membership in a labor organization as to authorize Congress to make it a crime against the United States for an agent of an interstate carrier to discharge an employee because of such membership on his part."[35]

There are a number of *dicta* of the United States Su-

[33] The point here made, to repeat, is that if Congress can legislate on grounds of public policy, its regulations must be connected with the use of the mails. The proposed legislation does not seem to fulfill this condition, for much, if not the greater part of the matter transmitted, would be harmless. It should be added, however (although the policy of the legislation is not here considered), that, conceding the power of Congress to act for the accomplishment of purposes not connected with the proper use of the mails, there are not unimportant economic objections to the proposed law. (Regulation of the Stock Exchange, p. 527 ff. and p. 585 ff.) These objections, I think, would have to be examined by the courts if Congress should be allowed the power which I have attempted to show it does not possess.

[34] 207 U. S. 463 (1907).

[35] Adair v. U. S., 208 U. S. 161 (1907); see also Keller v. U. S., 213 U. S. 138 (1908).

preme Court, particularly in regard to objectionable state statutes, which show that attempted indirect regulation is considered improper, at least for the local legislatures. First in time and importance comes Marshall's famous statement, that "should Congress under pretext of executing its powers, pass laws for the accomplishment of objects not entrusted to the government, it would become the painful duty of this tribunal, should a case requiring such a decision come before it, to say that such an act was not the law of the land."[36]

Or, as was said in another case: "The courts are not bound by mere forms, nor are they to be misled by mere pretenses. They are at liberty—indeed under a solemn duty—to look at the substance of things, whenever they enter upon the inquiry whether the legislature has transcended the limits of its authority. If, therefore, a statute purporting to have been enacted to protect the public health, the public morals, or the public safety, has no real or substantial relation to those objects, or is a palpable invasion of the rights secured by fundamental law, it is the duty of the courts to so adjudge and thereby give effect to the Constitution."[37] No power ought to be sought, much less adjudged, "in favor of the United States, unless it be clearly within reach of its constitutional charter." The courts are "not at liberty to add one jot of power to the national government beyond what the people have granted by the Constitution."[38]

The Court has, moreover, adhered to "the great principle that what cannot be done directly because of constitutional restriction, cannot be accomplished indirectly by legislation which accomplishes the same result. . . . Constitutional provisions," adds Justice Brewer, "whether operating by way of grant or limitation, are to be enforced according to their letter and cannot be evaded by any legislation which,

---

[36] McCulloch v. Maryland, 4 Wheat. 316 (1819).
[37] Mugler v. Kansas, 123 U. S. 623 (1887).
[38] Houston v. Moore, 5 Wheat. 1 (1820).

although not in terms trespassing upon the letter and spirit, yet in substance or effect destroys the grant or limitation."[39]

It is, moreover, a serious question whether arbitrary exclusions from the mails would not abridge the guarantee of due process of law. This question has never been before the Supreme Court of the United States, but a District Court has maintained that "the postal monopoly, if granted and exercised by a citizen or a corporation would, from the fact of its being a monopoly, make it imperative that all persons who paid the postal rates and conformed to the reasonable regulations of the postal service should have a common right to the use of the mails, and that, because of the fact of the monopoly thus granted. This right would be protected in the courts if the citizen or the corporation controlling the postal service should attempt to deprive him of it."

The court then suggests that if the federal government should become the owner of all transportation lines and establish a monopoly, facilities would have to be extended to all, subject "to such general laws and regulations as to rates and the operation of the lines as might be enacted and established"; that the right to travel and ship freight "would be readily recognized as a property right in the citizen and one of which a particular citizen could not be deprived except by due process of law. We think the right to the use of the mails, though in a degree much less valuable, than the use of the transportation lines, would be equally a property right, and one which could not be taken

[39] Fairbank v. U. S., 181 U. S. 283 (1901). In Union Bridge Co. v. U. S., 204 U. S. 364 (1907) this language was used: "If the means employed *have no substantial relation* to public objects which the government may legally accomplish, if they are arbitrary and unreasonable beyond the necessities of the case, the judiciary will disregard mere forms and interfere for the protection of rights injuriously affected by such illegal action. The authority of the courts to interfere in such cases is beyond all doubt." See also Morgan v. Louisiana, 118 U. S. 455 (1886); Postal Tel. Co. v. Adams, 155 U. S. 688 (1895); Collins v. New Hampshire, 171 U. S. 30 (1898), and Henderson v. The Mayor of New York, 92 U. S. 259 (1876).

away except by due process of law."[40] The use of this property right would, of course, be subject to police regulations by Congress, to the extent that they have been upheld by the Supreme Court, or to which this argument concedes that they may go,—always applying, however, directly to the *things* mailed.

One of the methods urged for compelling federal incorporation of trading companies engaged in interstate commerce is the denial of postal facilities to state chartered concerns, and concerning this one of the abler advocates of such an end, says: "If we are correct in believing that due process requires the equal protection of the laws, an arbitrary selection or classification is beyond the power of Congress. A law which divides those who use the mail into two general classes, all state corporations on the one hand, and all which are not incorporated by a state on the other, does not seem based upon any reasonable difference, either in the character of the person or in the kind of mail matter sent, which will make the classification more than arbitrary selection. The constitutionality of this method, therefore, seems open to grave question."[41] The conclusion of this writer, therefore, is that the constitutionality of the Pujo Bill would be open "to grave question" as denying due process of law.

Thus far the proposed extension of federal control by forbidding persons to use the mails, has been objected to as (in the suggested bill at least) abridging the freedom of the press, as not being a *bona fide* regulation of the mails, as attempting to obviate the objection of *ultra vires* by the use of indirect means, and as denying due process of law. There is a final consideration, which, while not legally con-

[40] Hoover v. McChesney, 81 Fed. Rep. 472 (1897). "The right to mail matter was considered in Teal v. Felton [12 How. 284 (1851)], but was not established as a right peculiar to citizens." Lien, Privileges and Immunities of Citizens of the United States, p. 41 (Columbia University Studies in History, Economics and Public Law, vol. liv, no. 1). But it would not seem that this case considered such a subject.

[41] Heisler, Federal Incorporation, p. 86.

trolling, is none the less important. Without holding strictly to a "literary theory"[42] of the Constitution one can regret the apparently growing tendency to disregard constitutional provisions and to sanction all legislation if, by any twisted interpretation, it can be upheld by the courts, although it may, as in the case of the postoffice proposals considered above, be well outside the fairly considered powers of the law-making body. This tendency shows an impatience of legal restraint, and a disinclination to follow what may be called constitutional morality. The phrase is that of Grote,[43] who, describing Athenian Democracy in the time of Kleisthenes, emphasized the necessity for "a perfect confidence in the bosom of every citizen, amidst the bitterness of party contest, that the forms of the constitution will be no less sacred in the eyes of his opponents than in his own." Such constitutional morality he called "a natural sentiment" as it exists in the United States, but these words will no longer be true if Congress may extend its control in the manner proposed, without waiting for a grant of authority in the manner provided for by the Constitution.[44]

And if the courts should permit such extensions of federal control, enormous powers will, by judicial construction, be taken from the states and given over to the national legislature. For, as it is hardly necessary to remark, the denial of postal and interstate commerce facilities would be almost as efficacious as positive legislation; without using the mails and the channels of trade no business could successfully exist. If congressional control may be thus extended, every business and every individual needing to use the mails would become subject to federal regulation on the vague ground of public policy. The reserved powers of the states would then exist only by the sufferance of Congress, and the cardinal theory of the American system—that the federal government is one of enumerated powers—would become a cynical fiction.

[42] Woodrow Wilson, Congressional Government, p. 12.
[43] History of Greece, vol. ii, p. 86.
[44] But see Goodnow, Social Reform and the Constitution, p. 91 ff.

TABLE OF CASES

INDEX